TABLE OF CONTI

Top 15 Test Taking Tips

1. Know the test directions, duration, topics, question types, how many questions
2. Setup a flexible study schedule at least 3-4 weeks before test day
3. Study during the time of day you are most alert, relaxed, and stress free
4. Maximize your learning style; visual learner use visual study aids, auditory learner use auditory study aids
5. Focus on your weakest knowledge base
6. Find a study partner to review with and help clarify questions
7. Practice, practice, practice
8. Get a good night's sleep; don't try to cram the night before the test
9. Eat a well balanced meal
10. Wear comfortable, loose fitting, layered clothing; prepare for it to be either cold or hot during the test
11. Eliminate the obviously wrong answer choices, then guess the first remaining choice
12. Pace yourself; don't rush, but keep working and move on if you get stuck
13. Maintain a positive attitude even if the test is going poorly
14. Keep your first answer unless you are positive it is wrong
15. Check your work, don't make a careless mistake

Lesson 1

Place Value 1-100,000

 The place value of a digit is determined by where it is in a number.

Hundred Thousands	Ten Thousands	Thousands	Hundreds	Tens	Ones
1	2	3	4	5	6

123,456

One Hundred Twenty Three Thousand, Four Hundred Fifty Six

Write these numbers correctly in the blanks.

1. 422,719 =

4	2	2	7	1	9
Hundred Thousands	Ten Thousands	Thousands	Hundreds	Tens	Ones

2. 982,124 =

Hundred Thousands	Ten Thousands	Thousands	Hundreds	Tens	Ones

3. 263,927 =

Hundred Thousands	Ten Thousands	Thousands	Hundreds	Tens	Ones

4. 627,141 =

Hundred Thousands	Ten Thousands	Thousands	Hundreds	Tens	Ones

5. 891,362 =

Hundred Thousands	Ten Thousands	Thousands	Hundreds	Tens	Ones

Place Value Big numbers 1-1,000,000

The place value of a digit is determined by where it is in a number.

Millions	Hundred Thousands	Ten Thousands	Thousands	Hundreds	Tens	Ones
1	2	3	4	5	6	7

1,234,567

One million, two hundred thirty-four thousand, five hundred sixty-seven

---

1. 6,138,462 =

6	1	3	8	4	6	2
Millions	Hundred Thousands	Ten Thousands	Thousands	Hundreds	Tens	Ones

2. 3,194,675 =

Millions	Hundred Thousands	Ten Thousands	Thousands	Hundreds	Tens	Ones

3. 8,417,205 =

Millions	Hundred Thousands	Ten Thousands	Thousands	Hundreds	Tens	Ones

4. 2,765,447 =

Millions	Hundred Thousands	Ten Thousands	Thousands	Hundreds	Tens	Ones

5. 5,925,057 =

Millions	Hundred Thousands	Ten Thousands	Thousands	Hundreds	Tens	Ones

Lesson 2

Identifying Place Value - Word Problems

Solve the word problems below.

1. In the number 25,483 :
   A. This digit is in the ones place _____
   B. This digit is in the hundreds place _____
   C. The 5 is in the _____ place
   D. The 8 is in the _____ place

2. In the number 62,134 :
   A. This digit is in the tens place _____
   B. This digit is in the thousands place _____
   C. The 6 is in the _____ place
   D. The 4 is in the _____ place

3. In the number 84,327 :
   A. This digit is in the ones place _____
   B. This digit is in the thousands place _____
   C. The 2 is in the _____ place
   D. The 8 is in the _____ place

4. In the number 14,960 :
   A. This digit is in the hundreds place _____
   B. This digit is in the ten-thousands place _____
   C. The 0 is in the _____ place
   D. The 4 is in the _____ place

5. In the number 40,589 :
   A. This digit is in the ones place _____
   B. This digit is in the hundreds place _____
   C. The 0 is in the _____ place
   D. The 4 is in the _____ place

Lesson 4

Expanded Form

We learned earlier that every digit in a number has a place value. **Expanded form** shows that number expanded into an addition statement.

Example:

The expanded form of 5,786 is:
5,000 + 700 + 80 + 6.

Write each number in expanded form.

1.	82	2.	29	3.	56	4.	74
	80 + 2		_____		_____		_____

5.	35	6.	99	7.	250	8.	629
	_____		_____		_____		_____

9.	150	10.	892	11.	905	12.	427
	_____		_____		_____		_____

13. Twenty - Nine

20 + 9

14. Seventy - One

_____

15. Eighty - Six

_____

16. Fifty - Four

_____

17. Sixteen

_____

18. Thirty - Eight

_____

- 11 -

Expanded Form 2

Write each number in expanded form.

1. 156   **2.** 658   **3.** 295   **4.** 431

_____ _____ _____ _____

5. 567   **6.** 155   **7.** 832   **8.** 394

_____ _____ _____ _____

9. 2,591   **10.** 8,942   **11.** 4,154

_____ _____ _____

12. 6,387   **13.** 1,582   **14.** 3,578

_____ _____ _____

15. 44,658   **16.** 73,435

_____ _____

17. 95,261   **18.** 37,872

_____ _____

Lesson 5

Ordering up to 10,000

Write these numbers in order from least to greatest.

1. 9,289 | 92,891 | 9,281 | 96,381   9,281   9,289   92,891   96,381

2. 23,112 | 23,111 | 22,311 | 2,313   _____

3. 7,856 | 7,855 | 78,855 | 78,856   _____

4. 11,112 | 1,111 | 11,131 | 10,112   _____

5. 4,326 | 44,326 | 44,436 | 4,316   _____

6. 3,289 | 3,891 | 3,819 | 3,818   _____

7. 57,289 | 57,891 | 57,211 | 57,500   _____

8. 60,255 | 6,552 | 66,252 | 6,255   _____

9. 15,247 | 15,250 | 15,248 | 15,249   _____

10. 9,564 | 92,564 | 9,546 | 93,564   _____

11. 8,219 | 84,921 | 84,218 | 84,219   _____

- 13 -

Ordering up to 100,000

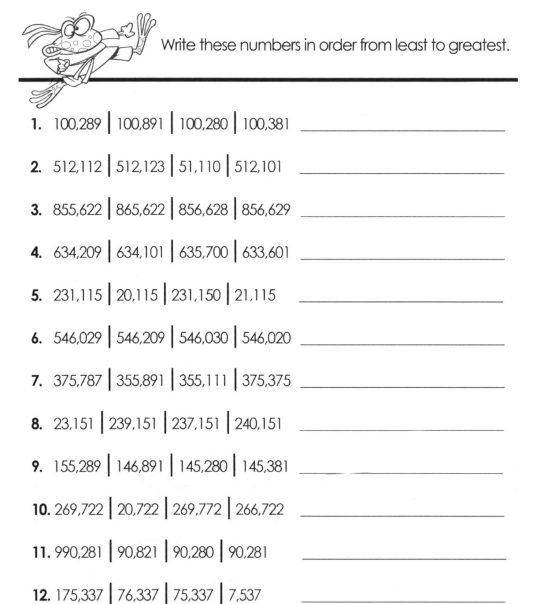

Write these numbers in order from least to greatest.

1. 100,289 | 100,891 | 100,280 | 100,381 _____

2. 512,112 | 512,123 | 51,110 | 512,101 _____

3. 855,622 | 865,622 | 856,628 | 856,629 _____

4. 634,209 | 634,101 | 635,700 | 633,601 _____

5. 231,115 | 20,115 | 231,150 | 21,115 _____

6. 546,029 | 546,209 | 546,030 | 546,020 _____

7. 375,787 | 355,891 | 355,111 | 375,375 _____

8. 23,151 | 239,151 | 237,151 | 240,151 _____

9. 155,289 | 146,891 | 145,280 | 145,381 _____

10. 269,722 | 20,722 | 269,772 | 266,722 _____

11. 990,281 | 90,821 | 90,280 | 90,281 _____

12. 175,337 | 76,337 | 75,337 | 7,537 _____

Lesson 6

Number Patterns to 10,000

Complete the number patterns.

1.   10,475 | 10,485 | __10,495__ | __11,005__

2.   98,211 | _____ | _____ | 98,511

3.   _____ | 62,001 | _____ | 64,001

4.   22,729 | 22,829 | _____ | _____

5.   _____ | 82,657 | _____ | 84,657

6.   2,475 | 2,485 | _____ | _____

7.   11,303 | _____ | _____ | 14,303

8.   _____ | 42,370 | _____ | 44,370

9.   72,112 | 72,119 | _____ | _____

10. 33,776 | _____ | _____ | 36,776

12. _____ | 79,061 | _____ | 99,061

Number Patterns to 100,000

Complete the number patterns.

1. 980,211 | _____ | _____ | 980,511

2. _____ | 621,001 | _____ | 619,001

3. 282,729 | 282,829 | _____ | _____

4. _____ | 694,657 | _____ | 694,677

5. 111,729 | 112,729 | _____ | _____

6. _____ | 350,001 | _____ | 352,001

7. 523,303 | _____ | _____ | 526,303

8. _____ | 815,370 | _____ | 825,370

9. _____ | 256,119 | 356,119 | _____

10. 609,776 | _____ | _____ | 639,776

11. 110,383 | 115,383 | _____ | _____

12. 340,303 | _____ | _____ | 370,303

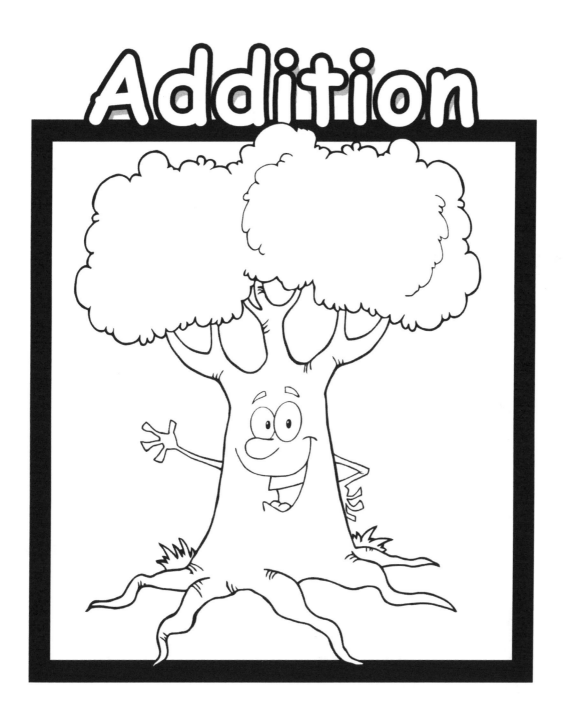

Lesson 1

2-Digit Addition - Regrouping 1

 To add multiple digit numbers together, start in the ones place and then use basic addition rules. When the number equals ten or more the first digit carries over to the next spot. This is called **regrouping**.

	Hundreds	Tens	Ones
Step 1: Add the digits in the ones column.		8	5
	+ 1	7
			[2]

	Hundreds	Tens	Ones
Step 2: Carry the 1 over to the top of the tens column.		1	
	x	8	5
	1	7
		①	2

	Hundreds	Tens	Ones
Step 3: Add all the digits in the tens column together.		1 +	
	x	8	5
	↓1	7
	[1]	[0]	2

Solve the problems below.

1. 4 9
     + 3 2
     ─────
      8 1

2. 5 8
     +   7
     ─────

3. 8 3
     + 8 4
     ─────

4. 4 2
     +   9
     ─────

5. 5 2
     + 7 2
     ─────

6. 4 4
     +   5
     ─────

7. 3 2
     + 1 4
     ─────

8. 1 8
     + 2 0
     ─────

9. 7 1
     + 9 2
     ─────

10. 5 9
      +   6
      ─────

11. 8 1
      +   9
      ─────

12. 6 0
      + 5 7
      ─────

13. 3 2
      + 4 0
      ─────

14. 1 9
      +   2
      ─────

15. 2 7
      + 8 6
      ─────

2-Digit 3-Row Addition - Regrouping 2

To add multiple digit numbers together, start in the ones place and then use basic addition rules. When the number equals ten or more the first digit carries over to the next spot. This is called **regrouping**.

Solve the problems below.

1. 12	2. 72	3. 72	4. 30	5. 23
60	44	16	82	67
+ 42	+ 55	+ 11	+ 8	+ 94

6. 50	7. 24	8. 81	9. 96	10. 75
32	72	12	64	11
+ 86	+ 39	+ 4	+ 51	+ 70

11. 44	12. 88	13. 20	14. 99	15. 60
79	52	36	85	92
+ 93	+ 6	+ 24	+ 13	+ 41

16. 30	17. 77	18. 10	19. 92	20. 17
57	12	28	68	29
+ 94	+ 9	+ 96	+ 47	+ 3

Lesson 4

Addition Word Problems

Use addition to solve the problems below.

1. Elle picked apples for four days. On day one she picked 10 apples. On day two she picked 26 apples. On day three she picked 14 apples. On day four she picked 14 apples. How many apples does Elle have in total?

_____

2. Cindy has been doing her chores every day after school. On Monday she swept the floor for 12 minutes. On Tuesday she spent 9 minutes making her bed. On Wednesday she washed the dishes for 20 minutes. On Thursday she spent 15 minutes vacuuming the floor. How much time did she spend on her chores?

_____

3. Steven is good at basketball. In game one he scored 14 points. In game two he scored 22 points. In game three he scored 27. In games four and five he scored 17 and 12 points. How many points has Steven scored so far?

_____

4. Amy loves to read. She reads every day after school. One day she read 45 minutes. The next day she read 30 minutes. The day after that she spent 57 minutes reading. Yesterday she read for 26 minutes and today she spent 15 minutes reading her book. How much time has she spent reading this week?

_____

Lesson 5

3-Digit Addition - Regrouping 1

To add multiple-digit numbers together, start in the ones place and then use basic addition rules. When a number equals ten or more the first digit carries over to the next spot. This is called **regrouping**.

Step 1: Add the digits in the one's column and carry over the 1 to the ten's column.	Step 2: Next add the digits in the tens's column and carry over the 1 to the hundred's column.	Step 3: Next add the digits in the hundred's column.	Step 4: Finally, carry over the 1 from the hundred's column to the thousands's column.

Step 1:

1000's	100's	10's	1's
		1	
	6	4	3
+	5	8	9
			[2]

Step 2:

1000's	100's	10's	1's
	1	1	
	6	4	3
+	5	8	9
	[3]	2	

Step 3:

1000's	100's	10's	1's
	1	1	
	6	4	3
+	5	8	9
[2]	3	2	

Step 4:

1000's	100's	10's	1's
	1	1	
	6	4	3
+	5	8	9
[1]	2	3	2

Solve the problems below. Use regrouping when needed.

1. 498
   +321
   ———
    819

2. 580
   +729

3. 134
   + 22

4. 309
   +447

5. 253
   +203

6. 171
   + 82

7. 344
   +493

8. 714
   +507

9. 629
   + 78

10. 629
   +351

3-Digit Addition - Regrouping 2

Solve the problems below using regrouping.

1. 151
   +459

2. 239
   +205

3. 677
   +380

4. 406
   +312

5. 951
   +123

6. 705
   +357

7. 824
   +199

8. 901
   +699

9. 333
   +178

10. 101
    +752

11. 509
    +456

12. 712
    + 55

13. 278
    +333

14. 158
    +207

15. 199
    +682

16. 999
    +715

17. 508
    +349

18. 724
    +924

19. 911
    +667

20. 507
    +133

Lesson 6

3-Digit 3-Row Addition - Regrouping

To add multiple digit numbers together, start in the ones place and then use basic addition rules. When the number equals ten or more the first digit carries over to the next spot. This is called **regrouping**.

Solve the problems below using regrouping.

1.   2 0 9
      1 5 8
   + 4 7 2
   ———
      8 3 9
	2. 4 5 6
	          4 1
	   + 1 3 7
		3. 6 5 2
		      1 8 9
		   + 3 0 5
			4. 5 7 2
			      2 6 7
			   + 4 5 3
				5. 7 1 1
				      2 0 9
				   + 3 7 4

6.   4 5 5
      1 2 6
   + 9 0 7
	7. 5 0 1
	      4 7 2
	   + 9 0 4
		8. 7 8 2
		      1 0 6
		   + 3 1 3
			9. 9 5 5
			      5 7 2
			   + 1 1 7
				10. 3 8 9
				       4 1 1
				    + 3 5 4

11.   1 1 1
       6 8 4
    + 2 4 3
	12. 2 5 4
	       9 0 6
	    + 1 4 5
		13. 7 1 5
		       3 5 5
		    + 7 4 2
			14. 7 4 2
			       2 7 9
			    + 1 0 9
				15. 9 5 8
				       1 4 4
				    + 3 0 2

16.   6 2 1
       4 3 5
    + 9 0 5
	17. 3 2 2
	       5 3 2
	    + 8 1 4
		18. 7 5 2
		       9 6 2
		    + 1 0 3
			19. 8 8 4
			       2 2 2
			    + 6 0 6
				20. 3 0 8
				       1 4 4
				    + 7 2 2

3-Digit 3-Row Addition - Regrouping 2

To add multiple digit numbers together, start in the ones place and then use basic addition rules. When the number equals ten or more the first digit carries over to the next spot. This is called **regrouping**.

Solve the problems below using regrouping.

1. 643 207 + 318	**2.** 119 875 + 40	**3.** 307 458 + 156	**4.** 678 152 + 306	**5.** 819 644 + 278
6. 339 107 + 389	**7.** 712 263 + 140	**8.** 181 396 + 15	**9.** 899 295 + 590	**10.** 165 980 + 263
11. 752 310 + 726	**12.** 157 682 + 898	**13.** 208 489 + 912	**14.** 257 367 + 6	**15.** 700 973 + 275
16. 661 894 + 64	**17.** 313 578 + 149	**18.** 985 405 + 123	**19.** 785 246 + 385	**20.** 222 746 + 118

Lesson 7

4-Digit Addition - Regrouping

Solve the problems below using regrouping.

1. 6 8 9 5
    + 5 4 0 6
    ‾‾‾‾‾‾‾‾‾
    1 2 3 0 1

2. 1 2 5 9
    + 9 5 0 2

3. 9 5 4 3
    + 7 8 4 5

4. 4 0 5 1
    + 1 1 5 0

5. 8 5 0 7
    + 9 8 4 7

6. 3 2 5 0
    +   4 0 6

7. 2 4 7 0
    + 3 3 5 7

8. 1 5 8 9
    + 6 8 7 5

9. 5 5 7 9
    + 6 0 7 7

10. 1 0 8 9
    + 2 7 8 6

11. 7 7 5 0
    +   5 9 7

12. 3 3 7 8
    + 4 5 0 8

13. 6 9 1 7
    + 7 5 0 2

14. 4 3 2 9
    +   9 9 9

15. 9 9 4 8
    +   1 1 3

16. 4 7 0 5
    + 4 8 6 6

17. 1 5 8 0
    + 3 9 8 7

18. 2 7 7 8
    + 4 8 9 1

19. 5 5 7 6
    +   5 6 9

20. 3 5 2 0
    + 1 3 3 9

Lesson 8

4-Digit 3-Row Addition - Regrouping

Solve the problems below using regrouping.

1. 1091
   2157
   +3267
   ___
   6515

2. 9815
   4803
   +2216
   ___

3. 3891
   1259
   +7520
   ___

4. 2552
   8406
   +2271
   ___

5. 5330
   1211
   +9801
   ___

6. 4881
   2009
   +1987
   ___

7. 3072
   1650
   +1578
   ___

8. 1985
   8105
   +1776
   ___

9. 9841
   2750
   +1349
   ___

10. 5400
    7501
    +3814
    ___

11. 7072
    6152
    +1785
    ___

12. 1707
    1804
    +2950
    ___

13. 2400
    3962
    +8815
    ___

14. 6074
    1255
    +8079
    ___

15. 8180
    2755
    +2577
    ___

16. 9064
    9607
    +6074
    ___

17. 4911
    2757
    +3025
    ___

18. 5787
    6962
    +1570
    ___

19. 7705
    5321
    +1766
    ___

20. 3033
    1447
    +9632
    ___

Lesson 9

5-Digit Addition - Regrouping

Solve the problems below using regrouping.

1. 1 5,8 0 1
    + 3 5,8 4 7
    _____
    5 1 6 4 8

2. 7 5,2 1 1
    + 2 5,7 8 6
    _____

3. 8 9,0 5 7
    + 1 1,0 5 9
    _____

4. 3 3,5 2 0
    +   6,5 7 9
    _____

5. 4 0,5 1 7
    + 1 2,5 2 3
    _____

6. 7 4,2 5 9
    + 6 9,8 0 5
    _____

7. 9 4,5 2 1
    +   7,0 8 9
    _____

8. 3 0,6 7 1
    + 3 1,3 3 7
    _____

9. 4 5,9 9 4
    + 2 7,8 8 1
    _____

10. 6 5,8 1 7
    +   5,8 4 7
    _____

11. 1 1,0 7 2
    + 3 6,6 9 8
    _____

12. 3 2,5 0 1
    +   4,8 7 9
    _____

13. 9 0,1 1 7
    + 1 5,2 5 7
    _____

14. 8 5,0 2 4
    + 9 6,3 1 2
    _____

15. 5 7,7 8 1
    +   5,6 9 0
    _____

16. 7 8,5 2 1
    + 3 6,9 0 1
    _____

17. 5 8,5 2 0
    + 5 7,9 3 6
    _____

18. 3 0,2 5 8
    + 2 8,5 2 7
    _____

19. 7 8,2 6 9
    + 1 0,2 5 4
    _____

20. 6 3,3 9 1
    + 6 0,5 8 2
    _____

- 29 -

Lesson 10

5-Digit Addition – Regrouping 2

Solve the problems below using regrouping.

1. 6 8,5 0 2
    + 3 5,8 4 7
    _____

2. 3 2,0 0 0
    + 1 7,8 1 5
    _____

3. 4 9,2 1 5
    + 2 1,5 8 9
    _____

4. 6 5,1 0 7
    + 4 2,2 3 8
    _____

5. 8 6,0 1 1
    + 3 2,9 9 7
    _____

6. 9 1,0 5 8
    + 1 5,2 1 1
    _____

7. 7 0,1 2 2
    + 6 2,9 3 9
    _____

8. 2 9,0 0 6
    + 1 1,2 7 1
    _____

9. 5 5,1 2 7
    + 1 7,5 6 8
    _____

10. 2 5,0 8 7
    +   9,1 7 5
    _____

11. 4 9,1 8 6
    + 2 3,2 5 0
    _____

12. 9 5,1 1 8
    +   3,9 3 5
    _____

13. 7 7,1 1 7
    + 5 9,9 9 0
    _____

14. 4 5,7 1 0
    + 3 6,3 0 3
    _____

15. 6 7,1 8 1
    +   2,6 2 8
    _____

16. 8 2,2 0 7
    + 6 0,8 4 5
    _____

17. 4 5,3 8 7
    + 3 6,1 0 5
    _____

18. 7 7,0 0 7
    + 1 1,3 6 7
    _____

19. 6 0,1 1 7
    + 4 6,2 8 9
    _____

20. 8 4,9 9 9
    + 2 6,1 1 1
    _____

Lesson 1

2-Digit Subtraction - Borrowing 1

To subtract and borrow , start with the ones column. If the bottom number is of a greater value, you have to borrow from the next column.

Step 1: If the bottom number is a greater value than the top number, you need to borrow.	Tens	Ones	**Step 2:** Borrow 10 from the next column. Reducing the 8 to 7 and increasing 4 to 14. Now we are ready to subtract.	Tens	Ones	**Step 3:** Finish by subtracting the numbers in the tens column.	Tens	Ones
	8	⌐4¬		7 8̸	¹4		7 8̸	¹4
	- 1	⌊9⌋		- 1	9		- 1	9
					⌐5¬		⌊6⌋	5

Use borrowing to solve the problems below.

1.
   3 5
   - 6
   ———
   2 9

2.
   5 4
   - 2 8
   ———

3.
   8 3
   - 4
   ———

4.
   4 2
   - 1 5
   ———

5.
   5 6
   - 9
   ———

6.
   4 1
   - 5
   ———

7.
   8 2
   - 5 9
   ———

8.
   1 6
   - 7
   ———

9.
   7 1
   - 3
   ———

10.
   5 2
   - 2 8
   ———

11.
   8 7
   - 5 9
   ———

12.
   3 4
   - 6
   ———

13.
   7 2
   - 3 5
   ———

14.
   2 1
   - 2
   ———

15.
   9 1
   - 4 4
   ———

2-Digit Subtraction - Borrowing 2

Use borrowing to solve the problems below.

1.   4 4
  − 3 5

2.   6 4
  −   5

3.   3 7
  − 1 9

4.   6 6
  −   7

5.   5 5
  − 1 7

6.   5 0
  − 2 7

7.   8 8
  − 3 6

8.   2 5
  − 1 6

9.   7 2
  − 5 3

10.   3 2
  − 2 9

11.   4 4
  − 1 7

12.   9 0
  − 7 6

13.   2 9
  − 1 4

14.   6 5
  − 4 4

15.   7 8
  − 5 3

16.   6 3
  − 4 9

17.   5 0
  −   9

18.   3 7
  − 1 8

19.   9 9
  − 6 4

20.   5 2
  − 2 3

2-Digit Subtraction - Borrowing - Fill in the Blanks

Use borrowing to solve the problems below.

1. 4 8
   − 2 9
   ⎯⎯⎯
   1 ☐

2. 2 5
   − 7
   ⎯⎯⎯
   1 ☐

3. 6 0
   − ☐
   ⎯⎯⎯
   5 1

4. 3 6
   − 8
   ⎯⎯⎯
   ☐ 8

5. 7 7
   − ☐ 9
   ⎯⎯⎯
   5 8

6. 6 0
   − ☐ 3
   ⎯⎯⎯
   2 7

7. 9 4
   − 4 6
   ⎯⎯⎯
   ☐ 8

8. 1 5
   − 6
   ⎯⎯⎯
   ☐

9. ☐ 2
   − 9
   ⎯⎯⎯
   1 3

10. 3 0
    − 1 ☐
    ⎯⎯⎯
    1 3

11. 7 2
    − ☐ 4
    ⎯⎯⎯
    4 8

12. 2 0
    − ☐ 2
    ⎯⎯⎯
    8

13. 5 1
    − 1 6
    ⎯⎯⎯
    ☐ 5

14. 4 6
    − 9
    ⎯⎯⎯
    ☐ 7

15. 3 2
    − ☐ 9
    ⎯⎯⎯
    1 3

16. 6 7
    − 3 9
    ⎯⎯⎯
    ☐ 8

17. 1 2
    − ☐
    ⎯⎯⎯
    6

18. 2 4
    − ☐ 9
    ⎯⎯⎯
    5

19. 7 1
    − ☐ 5
    ⎯⎯⎯
    1 6

20. 4 7
    − 1 9
    ⎯⎯⎯
    ☐ 8

Lesson 2

Subtraction Word Problems

Use subtraction to solve the problems below.

1. Selena is a good soccer player. This season she has taken 38 shots at the goal and made 6 of them. How many shots has she missed this season?

_____

2. Billy just can't stop eating cookies. He had 62 cookies in his jar. He ate 18 of them. How many cookies are left in the jar?

_____

3. Aida loves baseball. She has gone to 103 games in her life. 39 were away games. How many were home games?

_____

4. Jonathan has collected 47 snowflakes today, but 23 of them have already melted. How many snowflakes does Jonathan have left?

_____

- 35 -

Lesson 3

3-Digit Subtraction - Borrowing 1

To subtract and borrow, start with the ones column. If the bottom number is of a greater value, you have to borrow from the next column.

Step 1:	Hundreds	Tens	Ones
Any time the bottom number in a column is of greater value than the top number, you need to borrow.	7	6	3
	− 4	8	5

Step 2:	Hundreds	Tens	Ones
Borrow 10 from the next column. This reduces the 6 to 5 and increases the numbers in the first column from 3 to 13.	7	5 ̷6	¹3
	− 4	8	5

Step 3:	Hundreds	Tens	Ones
Now we need to borrow 10 from the hundreds column. This reduces the 7 to 6 and increases the numbers in the tens column from 5 to 15.	6 ̷7	¹5 ̷6	¹3
	− 4	8	5

Step 4:	Hundreds	Tens	Ones
Finish by subtracting the numbers in all the columns.	6 ̷7	¹5 ̷6	¹3
	− 4	8	5
	2	7	8

Use borrowing to solve the problems below.

1. 289
− 134
___
155

2. 412
− 389

3. 518
− 79

4. 962
− 473

5. 412
− 273

6. 652
− 386

7. 179
− 83

8. 712
− 554

9. 369
− 254

10. 811
− 632

11. 895
− 67

12. 337
− 287

13. 615
− 457

14. 906
− 687

15. 675
− 399

3-Digit Subtraction - Borrowing 2

 Use borrowing to solve the problems below.

1. 2 9 6
  - 1 4 7

2. 4 7 2
  - 2 2 8

3. 9 1 5
  - 4 5 5

4. 3 7 1
  -   5 2

5. 6 1 2
  - 3 7 7

6. 5 0 1
  - 4 5 8

7. 7 1 5
  - 2 0 7

8. 1 8 5
  - 1 5 2

9. 9 9 9
  - 3 4 2

10. 3 0 7
   - 1 5 8

11. 8 4 4
   - 5 9 9

12. 1 9 9
   -   5 7

13. 6 8 9
   - 3 9 4

14. 4 7 2
   -   5 9

15. 3 1 5
   - 1 9 9

16. 5 7 8
   - 4 1 9

17. 9 7 2
   - 8 5 9

18. 5 7 2
   - 2 8 9

19. 9 1 1
   - 4 8 7

20. 3 0 8
   - 1 5 7

3-Digit Subtraction - Borrowing - Fill in the Blanks

Use borrowing to fill in the blanks below.

1.   428
   − 305
   ‾‾‾‾‾
   1☐3

2.   577
   − ☐07
   ‾‾‾‾‾
   370

3.   671
   − 1☐5
   ‾‾‾‾‾
   486

4.   780
   − 339
   ‾‾‾‾‾
   ☐41

5.   719
   − 45☐
   ‾‾‾‾‾
   267

6.   672
   − ☐35
   ‾‾‾‾‾
   537

7.   517
   − 365
   ‾‾‾‾‾
   1☐2

8.   217
   − 82
   ‾‾‾‾‾
   13☐

9.   857
   − 369
   ‾‾‾‾‾
   4☐8

10.   624
   − 29
   ‾‾‾‾‾
   ☐95

11.   78☐
   − 345
   ‾‾‾‾‾
   440

12.   266
   − 117
   ‾‾‾‾‾
   1☐9

13.   456
   − 3☐5
   ‾‾‾‾‾
   141

14.   206
   − 12☐
   ‾‾‾‾‾
   85

15.   367
   − 27☐
   ‾‾‾‾‾
   92

16.   785
   − 316
   ‾‾‾‾‾
   46☐

17.   454
   − ☐99
   ‾‾‾‾‾
   255

18.   720
   − 367
   ‾‾‾‾‾
   ☐53

19.   894
   − 176
   ‾‾‾‾‾
   7☐8

20.   269
   − ☐56
   ‾‾‾‾‾
   113

Lesson 4

4-Digit Subtraction - Borrowing 1

 Use what you learned about borrowing to
solve the problems below.

1. 6,432
   − 5,320
   _____
   1,112

2. 2,675
   − 1,564
   _____

3. 4,233
   −   452
   _____

4. 5,428
   − 2,649
   _____

5. 1,995
   −   239
   _____

6. 7,321
   −   834
   _____

7. 9,211
   − 1,700
   _____

8. 3,946
   − 1,682
   _____

9. 2,463
   − 1,939
   _____

10. 8,959
    − 3,274
    _____

11. 1,295
    −   968
    _____

12. 9,942
    − 7,895
    _____

13. 7,542
    − 2,907
    _____

14. 3,649
    − 1,590
    _____

15. 9,864
    − 4,389
    _____

16. 3,888
    −   999
    _____

17. 5,001
    − 3,547
    _____

18. 1,775
    −   859
    _____

19. 3,880
    − 1,125
    _____

20. 9,567
    − 6,820
    _____

4-Digit Subtraction - Borrowing 2

Use what you learned about borrowing to
solve the problems below.

1. 3,2 9 1
  − 1,6 7 5

2. 7,0 5 2
  − 5,8 9 4

3. 1,0 2 0
  −   5 3 2

4. 9,2 1 4
  − 7,5 8 0

5. 2,8 5 6
  − 1,6 9 7

6. 5,4 4 1
  − 2,5 8 3

7. 7,6 5 4
  − 5,4 3 9

8. 9,2 0 1
  − 2,5 5 0

9. 6,5 4 9
  − 3,0 5 8

10. 1,2 0 5
  −   3 1 7

11. 4,0 5 3
  − 1,5 8 9

12. 9,0 8 7
  − 4,6 8 2

13. 3,0 0 1
  − 1,8 9 2

14. 9,8 9 7
  − 5,4 3 2

15. 6,9 0 1
  − 3,7 8 4

16. 5,3 3 8
  − 2,0 5 8

17. 8,0 7 1
  − 3,6 8 7

18. 9,0 0 1
  − 5,5 9 2

19. 4,2 0 7
  − 2,0 7 2

20. 9,9 9 1
  − 3,0 5 8

Lesson 5

5-Digit Subtraction - Borrowing 1

Use what you learned about borrowing to solve the problems below.

1. 62,734
    − 49,586
    _____
    13,148

2. 45,689
    − 29,875
    _____

3. 90,254
    − 67,702
    _____

4. 12,097
    − 7,850
    _____

5. 80,775
    − 24,078
    _____

6. 37,820
    − 9,507
    _____

7. 54,519
    − 20,179
    _____

8. 70,421
    − 34,219
    _____

9. 21,997
    − 1,509
    _____

10. 95,327
    − 70,587
    _____

11. 40,871
    − 27,815
    _____

12. 10,037
    − 5,871
    _____

13. 78,510
    − 40,327
    _____

14. 37,540
    − 1,058
    _____

15. 50,574
    − 27,899
    _____

16. 29,992
    − 10,871
    _____

17. 40,087
    − 21,589
    _____

18. 78,560
    − 52,278
    _____

19. 12,687
    − 11,339
    _____

20. 45,230
    − 7,854
    _____

5-Digit Subtraction - Borrowing 2

Use what you learned about borrowing to solve the problems below.

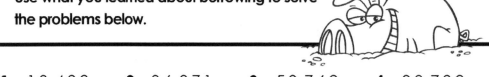

1. 13,489
    - 11,792

2. 86,371
    - 45,927

3. 50,762
    - 36,875

4. 38,792
    - 15,806

5. 21,743
    - 6,158

6. 35,309
    - 9,507

7. 98,051
    - 65,473

8. 66,259
    - 29,402

9. 32,278
    - 14,369

10. 20,897
    - 5,098

11. 55,807
    - 34,568

12. 97,051
    - 65,204

13. 65,790
    - 22,903

14. 10,854
    - 9,661

15. 77,059
    - 40,572

16. 85,220
    - 33,078

17. 36,754
    - 18,265

18. 54,587
    - 33,058

19. 63,017
    - 45,582

20. 70,000
    - 25,783

Lesson 1

Adding Decimals 1

Adding decimals is like most normal addition. You just have to remember to line up the decimals.

Hint: Decimal points always go at the end of a whole number (3 = 3.0 or 3.00)

	Example: Add 2.43, 4.5 and 3	
Step 1: Line up the numbers	**Step 2:** Add zeros	**Step 3:** Find the total
2.43 4.5 + 3	2.43 4.50 + 3.00	2.43 4.50 + 3.00 9.93

Line up the numbers and solve the problems below.
Show your work in the boxes.

1: 1.21 + 2.33 + .05   **2:** 4 + 1.63 + 2.20   **3:** .24 + 4.87 + 11

```
  1.21
  2.33
+  .05
  3.59
```

4: 7.12 + 2.04 + 5   **5:** 9.11 + .43 + .89   **6:** 64 + 8.79 + 1.57

Adding Decimals 2

Use what you learned about adding numbers with decimals to find the totals to the questions below. Show your work in the boxes.

1:   9.34 + .44 + 6.17   **2:**   590 + 2.49 + 71.99   **3:**   .04 + 3.03 + 24.42

4:   3.18 + 2.01 + 35.78   **5:**   584.11 + 789.8 + .50   **6:**   584 + 1.29 + 36.99

7:   6.08 + 3.46 + .99   **8:**   15 + 37.16 + 2.09   **9:**   7.89 + 1.11 + 109

Lesson 2

Adding Money 1

 The rules that we learned for adding decimals is how we add money.

```
   2.69          $2.69
+  5.11    =   + $5.11
-------        --------
   7.80          $7.80
```

Find the totals below.

1. $1.40
  + $3.63
  $5.03

2. $7.18
  + $4.45

3. $2.50
  + $6.72

4. $1.15
  + $5.25

5. $9.40
  + $3.35

6. $10.45
  +$11.82

7. $20.15
  + $2.38

8. $14.05
  + $5.59

9. $6.55
  $1.47
  + $3.91

10. $2.13
  $4.75
  + $5.59

11. $1.55
  $8.09
  + $6.32

12. $2.77
  $8.59
  + $3.40

13. $17.09
  $1.99
  + $3.20

14. $10.33
  $8.95
  + $1.27

15. $18.17
  $9.49
  + $7.55

16. $12.35
  $2.78
  + $5.15

Adding Money 2

Find the totals below.

1. $9.32
    + $4.13
    ───────
    $13.45

2. $6.91
    + $3.57

3. $8.10
    + $2.36

4. $5.55
    + $1.35

5. $77.02
    +$62.23

6. $50.85
    +$32.04

7. $29.77
    +$12.75

8. $82.26
    +$40.11

9. $16.88
    $91.05
    +$53.12

10. $55.30
     $30.99
     + $7.15

11. $62.10
     $1.99
     + $28.50

12. $39.03
     $20.27
     +$51.11

13. $100.33
     $55.70
     + $7.16

14. $555.46
     $71.26
     + $3.90

15. $123.50
     $40.49
     + $8.17

16. $609.99
     $24.35
     + $5.22

17. $759.09
     $208.99
     +$177.20

18. $405.00
     $620.50
     +$378.99

19. $907.89
     $182.63
     +$330.17

20. $365.11
     $657.78
     +$307.40

Adding Money 3

Find the totals below.

1. $6.05
  + $4.11

2. $3.94
  + $2.29

3. $9.99
  + $7.65

4. $5.25
  + $8.39

5. $8.38
  + $9.12

6. $66.45
  + $29.82

7. $95.30
  + $12.65

8. $84.94
  + $17.05

9. $29.75
    $1.40
  + $8.97

10. $20.51
    $45.68
  + $9.42

11. $95.12
    $58.63
  + $17.08

12. $62.22
    $30.52
  + $68.67

13. $152.78
  $126.36
 + $ 75.11

14. $429.33
  $639.95
 + $115.27

15. $290.24
  $907.57
 + $333.03

16. $369.67
  $105.18
 + $ 59.07

17. $625.99
  $470.75
 + $364.23

18. $129.00
  $650.70
 + $321.33

19. $459.99
  $630.01
 + $780.40

20. $111.27
  $252.96
 + $639.57

Lesson 3

Adding Decimals Word Problems

Solve the problems below.

1. Jimmie's water gun can hold 30.08 ounces of water. Steven's water gun can hold 22.56 ounces. How many ounces of water do they have together?

_____

2. Sara walks every afternoon. On Monday she walked 2.3 miles. On Tuesday she walked 1.8 miles. On Wednesday she walked 3.1 miles. How many miles did she walk in total?

_____

3. Mickey loves to race his bike. In race one he had a finishing time of 13.38 minutes. In race two he had a finishing time of 12.58 minutes. In race three he had a finishing time of 12.32 minutes. What was his total time for all the races?

_____

4. Mary can carry 6.75 pounds of dirt in her wagon. Mark can carry 8.25 pounds in his wagon. How much dirt can they carry in total?

_____

Lesson 4

Rounding Decimals 1

To round numbers with decimal points look at the numbers to right of the decimal. If it has a value of higher than 5 round the number to the left of the decimal up.

$$6.8 = 7$$

If the number to the right of the decimal is less than 5, round the number down.

$$6.3 = 6$$

Round each decimal to the nearest whole number.

1. 9 2.8 = <u>9 3</u>   2. 1 2.5 = ____

3. 3 3.1 = ____   4. 2 4.9 = ____

5. 5 7.7 = ____   6. 6 5.1 = ____

7. 8 2.5 = ____   8. 4 1.6 = ____

9. 6 8.6 = ____   10. 2 0.4 = ____

11. 3 4.2 = ____   12. 3 1.8 = ____

13. 7 6.7 = ____   13. 7 2.2 = ____

15. 1 2.3 = ____   16. 4 3.7 = ____

17. 4 5.8 = ____   18. 5 5.9 = ____

19. 2 1.4 = ____   20. 1 9.3 = ____

Rounding Decimals 2

Round each decimal to the nearest whole number.

1. 892.86 = _____   2. 112.51 = _____

3. 133.41 = _____   4. 24.9 = _____

5. 57.38 = _____   6. 765.12 = _____

7. 22.23 = _____   8. 341.64 = _____

9. 318.34 = _____   10. 920.48 = _____

11. 94.19 = _____   12. 31.83 = _____

13. 56.77 = _____   14. 672.26 = _____

15. 812.62 = _____   16. 543.71 = _____

17. 35.21 = _____   18. 811.95 = _____

19. 121.84 = _____   20. 698.34 = _____

Lesson 5

Subtracting Decimals 1

Subtracting decimals is like normal subtraction.
You just have to remember to line up the decimals.

Hint: Decimal points always go at the end of a whole number (6 = 6.0 or 6.00)

Example: Subtract 5.7 from 9.39

Step 1: Line up the decimals.	**Step 2:** Add zeros and borrow when needed.	**Step 3:** Subtract all the numbers.
9.39 − 5.7	8 9̶.¹39 − 5.70	8 9̶.¹39 − 5.70 3.69

Line up the numbers and solve the problems below.
Show your work in the boxes.

1. 6.05 - 3.89

```
  6.05
- 3.89
------
  2.16
```

2. 48.27 - 13.65

3. 8.55 - 3.9

4. 331 - 4.72

5. 902.22 - 47.79

6. 75.5 - 6.51

- 52 -

Subtracting Decimals 2

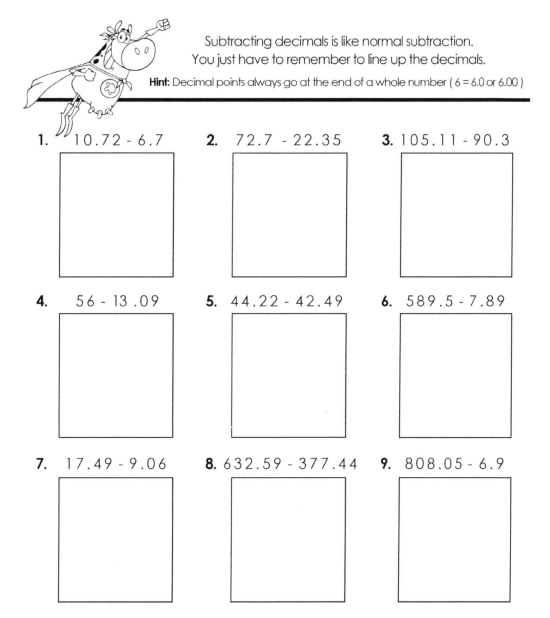

Subtracting decimals is like normal subtraction.
You just have to remember to line up the decimals.

Hint: Decimal points always go at the end of a whole number (6 = 6.0 or 6.00)

1. 10.72 - 6.7

2. 72.7 - 22.35

3. 105.11 - 90.3

4. 56 - 13 .09

5. 44.22 - 42.49

6. 589.5 - 7.89

7. 17.49 - 9.06

8. 632.59 - 377.44

9. 808.05 - 6.9

Lesson 6

Subtracting Money 1

Now that you know how to subtract decimals, use what you learned to answer these money problems.

6.89	$6.89
− 4.32 =	− $4.32
2.57	$2.57

Subtract the amounts below.

1. $4.58
   − $2.11
    $2.47

2. $8.49
   − $5.35

3. $6.50
   − $3.32

4. $9.75
   − $7.89

5. $9.90
   − $8.75

6. $2.93
   − $1.08

7. $6.15
   − $2.38

8. $7.38
   − $5.08

9. $4.15
   − $1.02

10. $5.65
   − $2.36

11. $3.46
   − $3.07

12. $9.15
   − $6.10

13. $13.04
   − $8.25

14. $31.35
   − $9.07

15. $15.89
   − $2.35

16. $17.38
   − $6.40

17. $16.82
   − $9.05

18. $21.93
   − $7.08

19. $10.15
   − $2.38

20. $20.00
   − $10.99

Subtracting Money 2

Subtract the amounts below.

1. $10.13
    − $2.29

2. $25.55
    − $5.02

3. $17.89
    − $3.39

4. $20.15
    − $7.09

5. $45.77
    − $15.36

6. $23.01
    − $17.99

7. $39.50
    − $27.28

8. $26.55
    − $11.17

9. $58.37
    − $49.99

10. $79.44
    − $60.76

11. $62.08
    − $34.13

12. $95.35
    − $17.37

13. $100.04
    − $68.68

14. $216.42
    − $84.36

15. $199.55
    − $35.23

16. $956.11
    − $25.71

17. $209.44
    − $155.88

18. $356.77
    − $208.05

19. $589.33
    − $199.07

20. $250.99
    − $217.95

Lesson 7

Subtracting Decimals Word Problems

Use subtraction to solve the problems below.

---

1. Pete wants a new teddy bear. His mom is going to help him buy one. A new bear costs $19.50. Pete has $7.32. How much money does he need to get from mom?

_____

2. Tammy wants a new jump rope. She has $3.78. The jump rope costs $6.99. How much more money does she need?

_____

3. Randy and John want a new toy truck. The toy truck costs $13.75. Randy has $4.15 and John has $6.42. How much more money do they need?

_____

4. Eric sold his old pogo stick for $5.89. A new one costs $35.99. How much more money does Eric need?

_____

Lesson 1

Multiplication

Multiplication Table

X	1	2	3	4	5	6	7	8	9	10
1	1	2	3	4	5	6	7	8	9	10
2	2	4	6	8	10	12	14	16	18	20
3	3	6	9	12	15	18	21	24	27	30
4	4	8	12	16	20	24	28	32	36	40
5	5	10	15	20	25	30	35	40	45	50
6	6	12	18	24	30	36	42	48	54	60
7	7	14	21	28	35	42	49	56	63	70
8	8	16	24	32	40	48	56	64	72	80
9	9	18	27	36	45	54	63	72	81	90
10	10	20	30	40	50	60	70	80	90	100

This is a **multiplication table**.
It shows how numbers multiply together.
The numbers in the **top row** multiply
by the numbers in the **left side row**.
Match up the rows to get your answer.

Lesson 2

Multiplication Tables 1

X	1	2	3
1	1	2	3
2	2	4	6

This is a multiplication table. Multiply the numbers in the top row by the numbers in the side row.

1.

X	1	2	3	4	5
6					
7					
8					

2.

X	7	8	9
4			
5			
6			
7			
8			

3.

X	9	10	11
7			
8			
9			
10			
11			

4.

X	2	3	4	5	6
20					
25					
27					

- 59 -

Lesson 3

Multiplying 1-Digit Numbers by 2-Digit Numbers

To multiply a one-digit number by a two-digit number,
start in the ones place and then use
basic multiplication rules.

	Tens	Ones
Step 1: Multiply the numbers in the ones place	4	3 ↑
	X	2
		[6]

	Tens	Ones
Step 2: Multiply the numbers in the tens place	4	3
	X↓	2
	[8]	6

Solve the problems below.

1. 2 4
    x 2
    -----
    4 8

2. 3 1
    x 3

3. 4 3
    x 2

4. 1 1
    x 7

5. 1 1
    x 5

6. 4 4
    x 2

7. 1 1
    x 9

8. 1 8
    x 1

9. 2 1
    x 4

10. 2 2
     x 3

Lesson 4

Multiplying by 10s

Multiplying by ten is just like regular two-digit number multiplication, but there is just one extra step. You bring the zero down first; this adds it to the end of the number.

Hundreds	Tens	Ones
	5	4
x	1	0
		[0]

Hundreds	Tens	Ones
	5	4
x	1	0
	[4]	0

Hundreds	Tens	Ones
	5	4
x	1	0
[5]	4	0

Solve the problems below.

1. 26
   x 10
   ———
   260

2. 71
   x 10

3. 67
   x 10

4. 22
   x 10

5. 38
   x 10

6. 84
   x 10

7. 19
   x 10

8. 18
   x 10

9. 94
   x 10

10. 29
   x 10

Multiplying by 10s 2

Multiplying by ten is just like regular two-digit multiplication, but there is just one extra step. You bring the zero down first; this adds it to the end of the number.

Solve the problems below by multiplying the numbers by ten.

1. 4 4
   x 1 0

2. 8 9
   x 2 0

3. 5 2
   x 5 0

4. 1 3
   x 9 0

5. 4 8
   x 3 0

6. 4 9
   x 2 0

7. 1 8
   x 1 0

8. 3 3
   x 8 0

9. 9 2
   x 5 0

10. 5 7
    x 7 0

11. 6 7
    x 1 0

12. 2 1
    x 6 0

13. 2 7
    x 1 0

14. 7 5
    x 9 0

15. 5 0
    x 3 0

16. 6 6
    x 2 0

17. 8 2
    x 1 0

18. 5 5
    x 3 0

19. 4 5
    x 5 0

20. 6 1
    x 9 0

Multiplying by 10 3

 Multiplying by ten is just like regular two-digit multiplication, but there is just one extra step. You bring the zero down first; this adds it to the end of the number.

Solve the problems below by filling in the blanks.

1. 82 x 10 = <u>820</u>   2. 59 x 10 = ____

3. 36 x 10 = ____   4. 91 x 10 = ____

5. 27 x 10 = ____   6. 60 x 10 = ____

7. 10 x 95 = ____   8. 10 x 89 = ____

9. 10 x 43 = ____   10. 10 x 27 = ____

11. 10 x 56 = ____   12. 10 x 39 = ____

13. ____ x 10 = 750   14. 12 x ____ = 120

15. 10 x ____ = 880   16. ____ x 10 = 620

17. ____ x 10 = 590   18. 10 x ____ = 10

- 63 -

Lesson 5

Multiplying 1-Digit Numbers by 2-Digit Numbers - Regrouping

To multiply a one-digit number by a two-digit number with regrouping, start in the ones place and then use basic multiplication rules. When the number equals ten or more, the first digit carries over to the next spot. This is called **regrouping**.

Step 1: Multiply the numbers in the ones column and carry the first digit over to the tens column.	Hundreds	Tens	Ones
		2	
	4	7	
x			3
			[1]

$3 \times 7 = 21$

Step 2: Multiply the digit in at the bottom of the ones column by the digit in the tens column and add the regrouped number.	Hundreds	Tens	Ones
		2 + 4	7
x			3
		[4]	1

$4 \times 3 = 12$ Then $12 + 2 = 14$

Step 3: The one then carries over to the hundreds place.	Hundreds	Tens	Ones
		2	
	4	7	
x			3
	[1]	4	1

Answer = 141

Solve the problems below.

1. 4 6
    x   2
    ——
    9 2

2. 5 8
    x   7
    ——

3. 4 3
    x   4
    ——

4. 8 7
    x   3
    ——

5. 3 6
    x   5
    ——

6. 4 4
    x   5
    ——

7. 3 2
    x   9
    ——

8. 5 5
    x   9
    ——

9. 9 9
    x   2
    ——

10. 5 9
    x   6
    ——

Multiplying 1-Digit numbers by 2-Digit numbers - Regrouping 2

To multiply a one-digit number by a two-digit number with regrouping, start in the ones place and then use basic multiplication rules. When the number equals ten or more the first digit carries over to the next spot. This is called **regrouping**.

Solve the problems below.

---

1. 2 8
    x 3

2. 7 5
    x 2

3. 1 3
    x 4

4. 6 2
    x 9

5. 9 9
    x 2

6. 8 5
    x 5

7. 2 6
    x 7

8. 4 4
    x 4

9. 9 6
    x 3

10. 5 7
     x 6

11. 7 2
     x 2

12. 3 3
     x 8

13. 8 2
     x 5

14. 2 9
     x 9

15. 6 6
     x 4

16. 5 9
     x 4

17. 2 6
     x 9

18. 5 4
     x 7

19. 9 5
     x 5

20. 4 6
     x 6

Lesson 6

Multiplying 1-Digit Numbers by 3-Digit Numbers - Regrouping

To multiply a one-digit number by a three-digit number, start in the ones place and then use basic multiplication rules.

	Hundreds	Tens	Ones
Step 1: First multiply the top digit in the ones column by the bottom digit in the ones column.	2	3	3
x			3
			9

3 x 3 = 9

	Hundreds	Tens	Ones
Step 2: Next multiply the digit in the tens column by the bottom digit in the ones column.	2	3	3
x			3
		9	9

3 x 3 = 9

	Hundreds	Tens	Ones
Step 3: Next multiply the digit in the hundreds column by the bottom digit in the ones column.	2	3	3
x			3
	6	9	9

2 x 3 = 6

Answer = 699

Solve the problems below.

1. 1 4 2
x   2
_____
2 8 4

2. 2 2 1
x   3

3. 3 4 1
x   2

4. 1 2 1
x   4

5. 6 9 8
x   1

6. 2 1 2
x   4

7. 1 3 2
x   3

8. 2 3 3
x   2

9. 2 3 2
x   3

10. 1 4 1
x   2

11. 2 1 2
x   3

12. 1 1 2
x   3

- 66 -

Multiplying 1-Digit numbers by 3-Digit numbers - Regrouping 2

To multiply a one-digit number by a three-digit number, start in the ones place and then use basic multiplication rules. Dont forget to use the regrouping rules you learned in the previous sections.

Solve the problems below.

1. 6 5 1
    x   2

2. 2 2 1
    x   3

3. 3 4 1
    x   5

4. 4 3 3
    x   4

5. 6 9 8
    x   9

6. 2 1 2
    x   4

7. 1 3 2
    x   3

8. 2 3 3
    x   8

9. 2 3 2
    x   9

10. 5 4 9
     x   2

11. 6 8 9
     x   7

12. 5 9 9
     x   5

13. 9 8 6
     x   8

14. 1 2 3
     x   6

15. 9 7 7
     x   4

16. 2 2 2
     x   5

17. 6 8 5
     x   4

18. 3 0 4
     x   8

19. 9 6 0
     x   9

20. 7 9 5
     x   2

Lesson 7

Multiplying 2-Digit numbers by 3-Digit numbers - Regrouping

To multiply a two-digit number by a two-digit number, start in the ones place and then use basic multiplication and addition rules. Dont forget to use what you learned about regrouping.

1. Multiply by the **ones** multiplier.	2. Multiply by the **tens** multiplier.	3. Add the products.

100's	10's	1's
	2 +	
	4	6
x	2	4
1	0	4

4 is the first multiplier
4 x 46 = 104

100's	10's	1's
	1 +	
	4	6
x	2	4
1	8	4
+ 9	2	0

20 is the second multiplier
20 x 46 = 104

100's	10's	1's
	4	6
x	2	4
1	8	4
+ 9	2	0
1 1	0	4

Add the two products
184 + 920 = 1104

Solve the problems below.

1.
```
   49
 x 15
 ----
  245
+490
 ----
  735
```

2.
```
   13
 x 12
 ----
```

3.
```
   54
 x 22
 ----
```

4.
```
   72
 x 45
 ----
```

5.
```
   38
 x 25
 ----
```

6.
```
   84
 x 55
 ----
```

7.
```
   69
 x 37
 ----
```

8.
```
   29
 x 23
 ----
```

9.
```
   79
 x 56
 ----
```

10.
```
   99
 x 56
 ----
```

Multiplying 2-Digit numbers by 3-Digit numbers - Regrouping 2

Solve the problems below.

1. 6 7
x 4 9

2. 2 4
x 1 5

3. 4 9
x 3 6

4. 2 9
x 2 7

5. 4 4
x 3 9

6. 8 4
x 6 0

7. 6 6
x 3 4

8. 8 7
x 1 1

9. 9 9
x 4 9

10. 7 0
x 5 9

11. 3 9
x 2 7

12. 2 4
x 1 7

13. 8 6
x 3 7

14. 1 1
x 8 3

15. 9 7
x 5 7

16. 5 5
x 9 0

17. 7 5
x 2 2

18. 6 8
x 4 3

19. 9 2
x 3 7

20. 1 9
x 2 6

Lesson 1

Division

- Division is a way to find out how many times one number is counted in another number.

- The ÷ sign means "divided by".

- Another way to divide is to use $\overline{)}$.

- The dividend is the larger number that is divided by the smaller number, the divisor.

- The answer of a division problem is called the quotient.

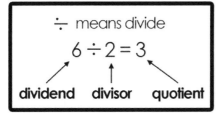

- 6 ÷ 2 = 3 is read "6 divided by 2 is equal to 3".

- In 6 ÷ 2 = 3, the divisor is 2, the dividend is 6 and the quotient is 3.

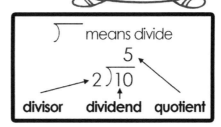

- $2\overline{)10}^{\,5}$ is read "10 divided by 2 is equal to 5".

- In $2\overline{)10}^{\,5}$, the divisor is 2, the dividend is 10 and the quotient is 5.

Lesson 2

Basic Division

Divide these problems.

1. $7\overline{)21}$ with 3 above

2. $6\overline{)48}$

3. $2\overline{)12}$

4. $7\overline{)28}$

5. $4\overline{)36}$

6. $3\overline{)21}$

7. $7\overline{)21}$

8. $5\overline{)40}$

9. $5\overline{)15}$

10. $2\overline{)6}$

11. $8\overline{)72}$

12. $10\overline{)100}$

13. $8\overline{)32}$

14. $5\overline{)25}$

15. $5\overline{)5}$

16. $8\overline{)88}$

17. $8\overline{)56}$

18. $5\overline{)75}$

19. $3\overline{)9}$

20. $4\overline{)32}$

Lesson 3

Division with Remainders 1

- Sometimes groups of objects or numbers cannot be divided into equal groups.
- The number left over in a division problem is called the remainder.
- The remainder must be smaller than the divisor.

If we divide 13 🍎 into groups of 5, you get 2 equal groups

and 3 🍎 left over. These are the **remainders**.

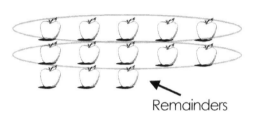

Remainders

This is how you write it out. →

$$\begin{array}{r} 2\,r\,3 \\ 5\overline{)13} \\ -10 \\ \hline 3 \end{array}$$

Divide these problems. Some may not have remainders.

1. $\begin{array}{r} 2\,r\,2 \\ 3\overline{)8} \\ -6 \\ \hline 2 \end{array}$

2. $7\overline{)35}$

3. $6\overline{)25}$

4. $8\overline{)39}$

5. $5\overline{)52}$

6. $9\overline{)85}$

7. $5\overline{)61}$

8. $3\overline{)43}$

Division with Remainders 2

Divide these problems. Some may not have remainders.

1. $2\overline{)9}$ 2. $6\overline{)15}$ 3. $2\overline{)33}$

4. $3\overline{)15}$ 5. $5\overline{)27}$ 6. $9\overline{)44}$

7. $9\overline{)58}$ 8. $7\overline{)32}$ 9. $6\overline{)40}$

10. $2\overline{)77}$ 11. $8\overline{)99}$ 12. $2\overline{)61}$

13. $8\overline{)66}$ 14. $5\overline{)62}$ 15. $8\overline{)49}$

Lesson 4

Division - Fill in the Blanks

Use division to fill in the boxes on the problems below.

1. 4)36̄ (9)

2. 6)□̄ (9)

3. 4)□̄ (15)

4. 5)□̄ (20)

5. 3)□̄ (2)

6. 7)□̄ (7)

7. 2)□̄ (5)

8. 9)□̄ (5)

9. 8)□̄ (8)

10. 9)□̄ (32)

11. 7)□̄ (9)

12. 3)□̄ (11)

13. 6)□̄ (9)

14. 4)□̄ (6)

Division - Fill in the Blanks 2

Use division to fill in the boxes on the problems below.

1. $8 \overline{)48}$ quotient 6

2. $\boxed{} \overline{)77}$ quotient 7

3. $\boxed{} \overline{)35}$ quotient 15

4. $\boxed{} \overline{)12}$ quotient 2

5. $\boxed{} \overline{)45}$ quotient 9

6. $\boxed{} \overline{)63}$ quotient 5

7. $\boxed{} \overline{)28}$ quotient 7

8. $\boxed{} \overline{)63}$ quotient 7

9. $\boxed{} \overline{)32}$ quotient 8

10. $\boxed{} \overline{)72}$ quotient 12

11. $\boxed{} \overline{)36}$ quotient 4

12. $\boxed{} \overline{)98}$ quotient 11

13. $\boxed{} \overline{)36}$ quotient 4

14. $\boxed{} \overline{)54}$ quotient 6

Lesson 5

Division Word Problems

Use division to solve the problems below.

1. Rachel bought three pairs of ballet shoes for $99. What is the cost of each pair of shoes?

_____

2. Charlie has 21 kids in his class. If he divides the kids into 3 groups how many kids will be in each group?

_____

3. Sara loves her dolls; she has 12 of them. If she divides them into groups of 4, how many dolls will be in each group?

_____

4. Harry has 72 toy trucks and cars. If he divides them into groups of 8, how many cars and trucks will be in each group?

_____

Lesson 6

2-Digit Quotients 1

Estimate	Divide the tens	Bring down the ones and repeat the steps.	The answer is: **23 r 3**
$\begin{array}{r} 2 \\ 4\overline{)95} \end{array}$	$\begin{array}{r} 2 \\ 4\overline{)95} \\ -8 \\ \hline 1 \end{array}$	$\begin{array}{r} 23 \\ 4\overline{)95} \\ -8\downarrow \\ \hline 15 \\ -12 \\ \hline 3 \end{array}$	Remember these steps: 1. Divide 2. Multiply 3. Subtract 4. Bring down
Take a look at the first digit. Estimate how many times 4 will go into 9 without going over the number.	4 can go into 9 twice. Multiply 4 x 2 and get 8. Subtract the 8 from 9 leaving 1.	Bring down the 5 from the one's column and repeat the steps. **The remainder is 3**	Repeat these steps until there are no more digits to bring down.

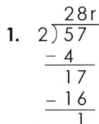

Divide these problems. Some may not have remainders.

1. $\begin{array}{r} 28\,r\,1 \\ 2\overline{)57} \\ -4 \\ \hline 17 \\ -16 \\ \hline 1 \end{array}$
2. $3\overline{)72}$
3. $4\overline{)65}$
4. $3\overline{)86}$

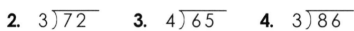

5. $2\overline{)37}$
6. $7\overline{)93}$
7. $5\overline{)73}$
8. $7\overline{)98}$

2-Digit Quotients 2

Divide these problems. Some may not have remainders.

1. 6)98   2. 3)65   3. 2)85   4. 4)99

5. 3)54   6. 6)77   7. 6)97   8. 2)59

9. 3)76   10. 2)46   11. 6)89   12. 3)44

Lesson 7

Dividing 3-Digit Numbers 1

When dividing a three-digit number by a two-digit number, the quotient may have two or three digits. Here are some examples:

Estimate		Divide
$\dfrac{200}{3\overline{)719}}$	→	239 r 2

3)719
- 6
11
- 9
29
- 27
2

1. Divide
2. Multiply
3. Subtract
4. Compare
5. Bring down

Repeat the steps as needed

Estimate		Divide
$\dfrac{70}{3\overline{)235}}$	→	78 r 1

3)235
- 21
25
- 24
1

1. Divide
2. Multiply
3. Subtract
4. Compare
5. Bring down

Repeat the steps as needed

Divide these problems. Some may not have remainders.

1. 246 r 3
4)987
- 8
18
-16
27
- 24
3

2. 6)297

3. 2)592

4. 3)769

5. 4)867

6. 5)934

- 80 -

Dividing 3-Digit Numbers 2

Divide these problems. Some may not have remainders.

1. 6) 987   2. 5) 857   3. 4) 827

4. 4) 359   5. 9) 289   6. 2) 764   7. 7) 357

8. 2) 923   9. 4) 577   10. 9) 956   11. 5) 234

12. 8) 649   13. 7) 937   14. 3) 899   15. 4) 521

Lesson 8

Averaging 1

An average is found by adding two or more quantities together and dividing by the number of quantities.

Step 1: Find the sum of the quantities ⟶ $35 + 15 + 10 = 60$

Step 2: Divide by the number of ⟶ $60 \div 3 = \text{\textcircled{20}}$
quantities

Work the problems out. Find the average of each set of numbers.

1. 6, 12, 15 = ___11___

      6
     12
  + 15
    33 ÷ 3 = ⑪

2. 1, 13, 9, 65 = _____

3. 2, 7, 11, 12 = _____

4. 48, 23, 28 = _____

5. 2, 29, 35, 18 = _____

6. 9, 33, 17, 29 = _____

- 82 -

Averaging 2

Find the average of each set of numbers.
Work the problems out.

1. 10, 62, 24 = _____

2. 28, 72, 44 = _____

3. 13, 51, 87, 65 = _____

4. 25, 78, 92, 13 = _____

5. 63, 32, 72, 90, 98 = _____

6. 100, 59, 87, 33, 21 = _____

- 83 -

Lesson 9

Averaging Word Problems

Write out each averaging problem and solve.

---

1. Jamie wants to know her average test score in math class. On her 4 tests she scored 79, 86, 92 and 80. What is her average test score?

_____

2. Steven scored 17, 16, 19, 27, 21 points in 5 games. How many points did he average?

_____

3. Kenny is good at video games. He played the game 6 times. He scored 128, 58, 166, 164, 212 and 72. What is his average score?

_____

Lesson 1

Flat Shapes

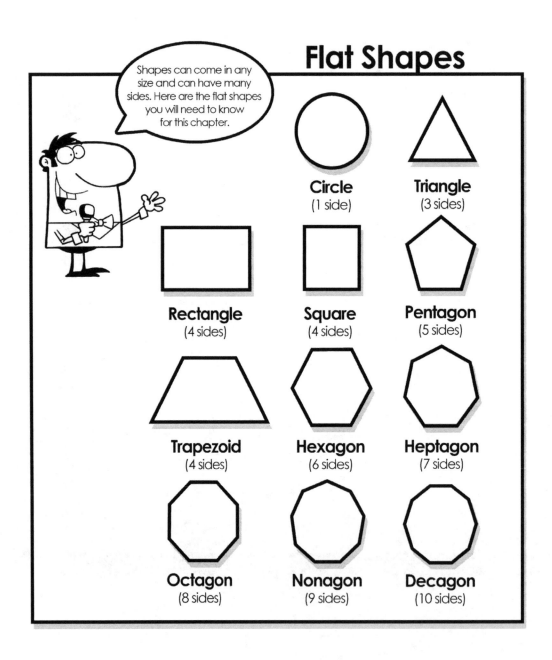

Identifying Flat Shapes

Write the number of sides in each box below.
Write the name of each shape in the blanks.

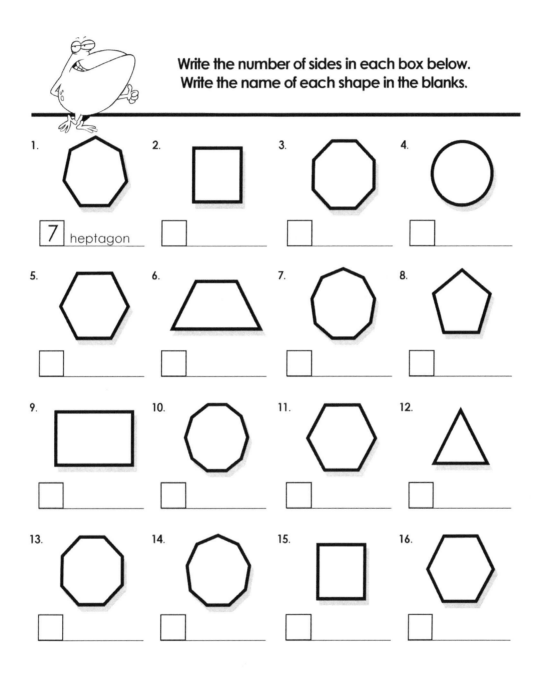

1.
[7] heptagon

2.
[ ]

3.
[ ]

4.
[ ]

5.
[ ]

6.
[ ]

7.
[ ]

8.
[ ]

9.
[ ]

10.
[ ]

11.
[ ]

12.
[ ]

13.
[ ]

14.
[ ]

15.
[ ]

16.
[ ]

Lesson 2

Solid Shape

Solid Shapes

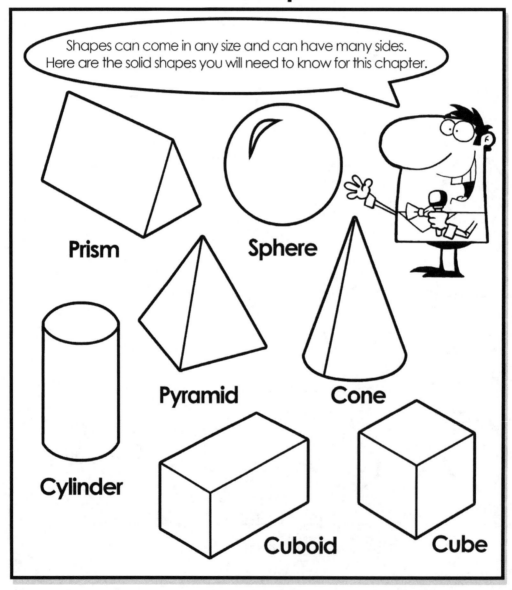

Shapes can come in any size and can have many sides. Here are the solid shapes you will need to know for this chapter.

Prism

Sphere

Pyramid

Cone

Cylinder

Cuboid

Cube

Identifying Solid Shape

Identify each shape below and write the
names in the blanks.

1.

cube
_____

2.

_____

3.

_____

4.

_____

5.

_____

6.

_____

7.

_____

8.

_____

9.

_____

10.

_____

11.

_____

12.

_____

13.

_____

14.

_____

15.

_____

16.

_____

Lesson 3

Identifying Triangles

Triangles can come in many shapes. Here are some examples.

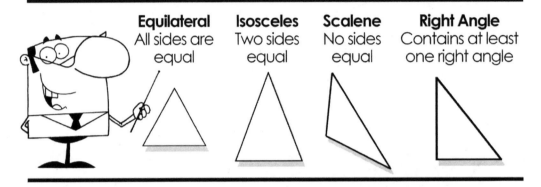

Equilateral	Isosceles	Scalene	Right Angle
All sides are equal	Two sides equal	No sides equal	Contains at least one right angle

Name each triangle as an **equilateral**, **isosceles**, **scalene** or **right** triangle.

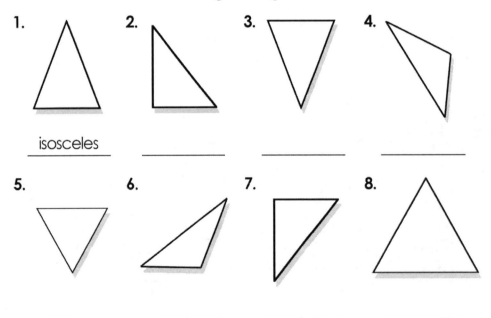

1.

isosceles

2.

3.

4.

5.

6.

7.

8.

Lesson 4

Identifying Points, Lines and Rays

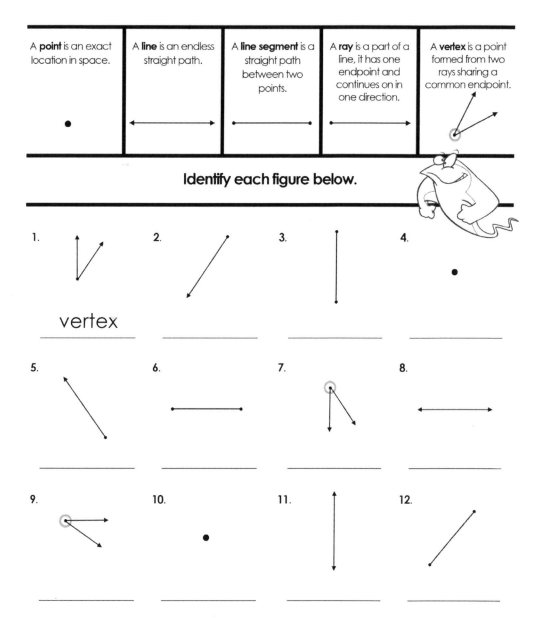

A **point** is an exact location in space.	A **line** is an endless straight path.	A **line segment** is a straight path between two points.	A **ray** is a part of a line, it has one endpoint and continues on in one direction.	A **vertex** is a point formed from two rays sharing a common endpoint.

Identify each figure below.

1.
vertex

2.

3.

4.

5.

6.

7.

8.

9.

10.

11.

12.

Lesson 5

Identifying Parallel and Perpendicular Lines

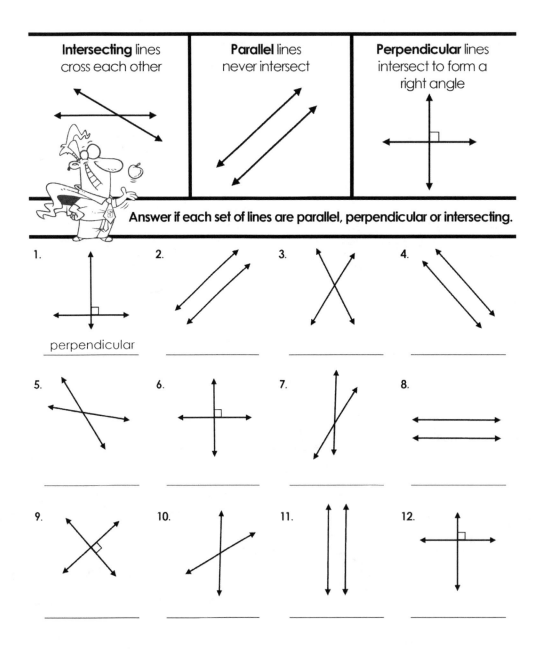

Intersecting lines cross each other

Parallel lines never intersect

Perpendicular lines intersect to form a right angle

Answer if each set of lines are parallel, perpendicular or intersecting.

1.

perpendicular

2.

_____

3.

_____

4.

_____

5.

_____

6.

_____

7.

_____

8.

_____

9.

_____

10.

_____

11.

_____

12.

_____

Lesson 6

Identifying Angles

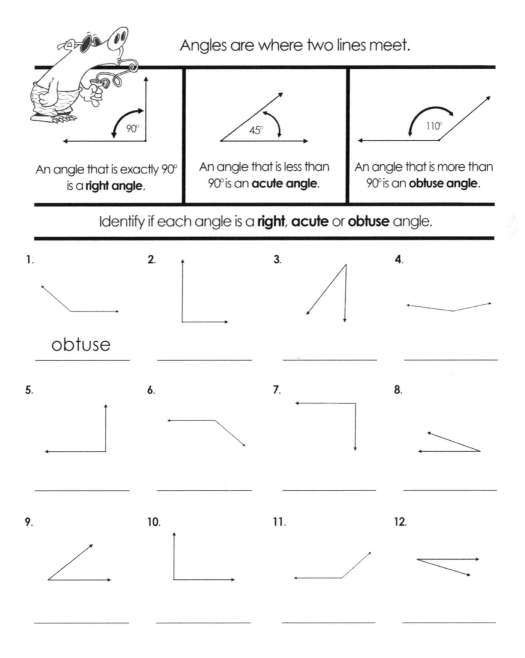

Angles are where two lines meet.

90°	45°	110°
An angle that is exactly 90° is a **right angle**.	An angle that is less than 90° is an **acute angle**.	An angle that is more than 90° is an **obtuse angle**.

Identify if each angle is a **right**, **acute** or **obtuse** angle.

1.

obtuse
_____

2.

_____

3.

_____

4.

_____

5.

_____

6.

_____

7.

_____

8.

_____

9.

_____

10.

_____

11.

_____

12.

_____

Lesson 7

Finding Area

Area is the measurement of a shape's surface area.
To find the **area** of a shape, multiply the length by the width.

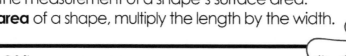

24 ft.

8 ft.

Area = 24 ft. x 8 ft. = 192 ft.
Area = 192 sq. ft.

Find the area of each shape. Write the problem out.

1.   6 in.

6 in.

2.   3 ft.

12 ft.

3.

21 in.   21 in.

6 x 6 = 36 sq. in.
_____

_____

_____

4.   4 ft.

25 ft.

5.

12 yd.   12 yd.

6.   9 in.

9 in.

_____

_____

_____

Lesson 8

Finding Perimeter 1

Perimeter is the distance around an object.
Find the perimeter of each object by adding all the sides.

12 in.

10 in.   10 in.   **Perimeter** = 12 in. + 12 in. + 10 in. + 10 in.

Perimeter = 44 in.

12 in.

Find the perimeter of each shape. Write the problem out.

1.
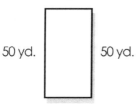
20 yd.
50 yd.   50 yd.
20 yd.

20 + 50 + 20 + 50 = 140yd.

2.
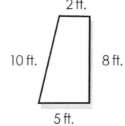
2 ft.
10 ft.   8 ft.
5 ft.

_____

3.
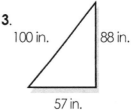
100 in.   88 in.
57 in.

_____

4.
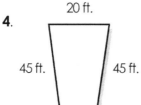
20 ft.
45 ft.   45 ft.
15 ft.

_____

5.
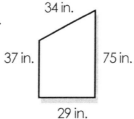
34 in.
37 in.   75 in.
29 in.

_____

6.
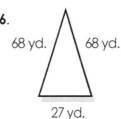
68 yd.   68 yd.
27 yd.

_____

- 95 -

Finding Perimeter 2

Find the perimeter of each shape.
Write the problem out.

1.
6 yd.
8 yd.
4 yd.

8 + 4 + 6 = 18yd.

2.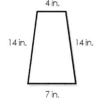
4 in.
14 in.
14 in.
7 in.

_____

3.
7 ft.
7 ft.
5 ft.
5 ft.
7 ft.
7 ft.

_____

4.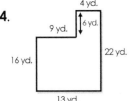
4 yd.
9 yd.
6 yd.
16 yd.
22 yd.
13 yd.

_____

5.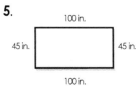
100 in.
45 in.
45 in.
100 in.

_____

6.
88 ft.
88 ft.
40 ft.

_____

7.
15 ft.
15 ft.
15 ft.
15 ft.

_____

8.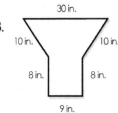
30 in.
10 in.
10 in.
8 in.
8 in.
9 in.

_____

9.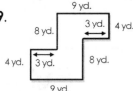
9 yd.
8 yd.
3 yd.
4 yd.
4 yd.
3 yd.
8 yd.
9 yd.

_____

Lesson 9

Understanding Volume 1

This cube is 1 ft long, 1 ft high and 1 ft wide. It has a volume of 1 cubic foot. ($1ft^3$).

1 ft. 1 ft. 1 ft.

When 4 of these cubes are put together, the new shape has a volume of 4 ft^3.

Find the volume of the shapes below.

1.

___3___ ft^3

2.

_____ ft^3

3.

_____ ft^3

4.

_____ ft^3

5.

_____ ft^3

6.

_____ ft^3

7.

_____ ft^3

8.

_____ ft^3

9.

_____ ft^3

Understanding Volume 2

Volume is the number of cubic units that can fit into a shape. To find volume, count the cubes or multiply length times width times height. *(L x W x H = volume)*

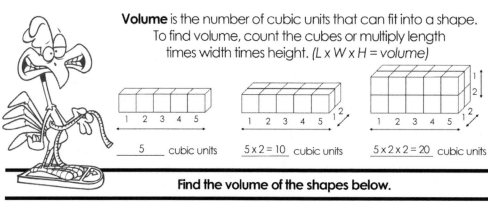

_____5_____ cubic units   _5 x 2 = 10_ cubic units   _5 x 2 x 2 = 20_ cubic units

Find the volume of the shapes below.

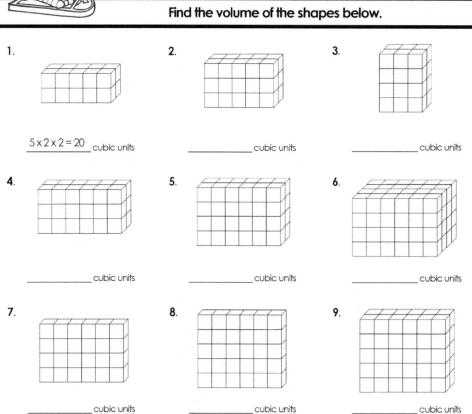

1.

_5 x 2 x 2 = 20_ cubic units

2.

_____ cubic units

3.

_____ cubic units

4.

_____ cubic units

5.

_____ cubic units

6.

_____ cubic units

7.

_____ cubic units

8.

_____ cubic units

9.

_____ cubic units

Understanding Volume 3

Volume is the number of cubic units that can fit into a shape. To find volume, multiply length times width times height.
(L x W x H = volume)

2 ft.
2 ft.
11 ft.

11 x 2 x 2 = 44 cubic feet

3 in.
3 in.
10 in.

10 x 3 x 3 = 90 cubic inches

Find the volume of the shapes below.

1.

5 in.
5 in.
20 in.

20 x 5 x 5 = 500 in.^{3}

2.
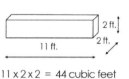
4 ft.
4 ft.
8 ft.

_____

3.
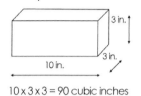
5 in.
8 in.
4 in.

_____

4.
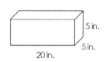
16 ft.
5 ft.
9 ft.

_____

5.

6 in.
4 in.
10 in.

_____

6.
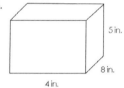
8 ft.
10 ft.
5 ft.

_____

7.

10 in.
9 in.
4 in.

_____

8.
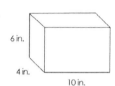
7 ft.
7 ft.
5 ft.

_____

9.
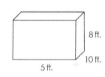
3 in.
6 in.
9 in.

_____

Lesson 1

Measurement

Capacity	Length	Weight
1 gallon = 8 pints	1 foot = 12 inches	1 pound = 16 ounces
1 gallon = 4 quarts	1 yard = 3 feet	1 ton = 2000 pounds
1 gallon = 16 cups	1 yard = 36 inches	1 ton = 32000 ounces
1 gallon = 128 fluid ounces	1 mile = 5280 feet	
1 quart = 4 cups	1 mile = 1760 yards	
1 quart = 2 pints		
1 pint = 2 cups		
1 cup = 8 fluid ounces		
1 pint = 16 fluid ounces		

Here are the measurements for **capacity**, **length** and **weight** you will need to know for this chapter.

Lesson 2

Ounces, Pounds and Tons Word Problems

Circle the correct answer for each question.

1. Lilly has grown a lot over the summer. How much does she weigh now?

   (60 pounds)   60 ounces   60 tons

2. Dad's new truck is very heavy; how much does it weigh?

   2 pounds   2 ounces   2 tons

3. Jan needs to sell more cookies to go on the trip. How many more cookies does she need to sell?

   5 pounds   5 ounces   5 tons

4. The pumpkin we grew is huge. How much does it weigh?

   37 pounds   37 ounces   37 tons

Ounces, Pounds and Tons

One - half pound (lb.) = 8 ounces (oz.)
1 pound (lb.) = 16 ounces (oz.)
One - half ton (T.) = 1,000 pounds (lb.)
1 ton (T.) = 2,000 pounds (lb.)

Complete the problems below.

 **1.** 48 oz. = _3_ lb.   **2.** 32 lb. = _____ oz.

 3. 4,000 lb. = _____ T. 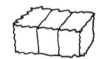 **4.** 80 oz. = _____ lb.

 5. 2 lb. = _____ oz.   **6.** 8 lb. = _____ oz.

 7. 3T. = _____ lb.   **8.** 6 lb. = _____ oz.

 9. 16 oz. = _____ lb.  **10.** 12,000 lb. = _____ T.

Lesson 3

Estimating Length

Circle the best unit of measurement to estimate each item's length.

1. Length of your foot.   (Inches)   Feet

2. Length of your house.   Inches   Feet

3. Length of your pen.   Inches   Feet

4. Height of your dad.   Inches   Feet

5. Length of your car.   Inches   Feet

6. Length of your hair.   Inches   Feet

Lesson 4

Inches, Feet and Yards

12 inches = 1 foot	3 feet = 1 yard
36 inches = 1 yard	

Compare inches to feet.

Use the symbols **<**, **>**, and **=** to answer the questions below

---

1. 10 feet **>** 100 inches   2. 20 inches ____ 3 feet

3. 12 inches ____ 1 foot   4. 6 feet ____ 50 inches

5. 40 inches ____ 3 feet   6. 5 feet ____ 70 inches

7. 4 feet ____ 48 inches   8. 72 inches ____ 6 feet

Compare inches, feet, and yards.

Use the symbols **<**, **>**, and **=** to answer the questions below

---

9. 9 feet ____ 32 yards   10. 46 inches ____ 2 yards

11. 40 feet ____ 3 yards   12. 4 yards ____ 15 feet

13. 4 feet ____ 100 inches   14. 1 foot ____ 2 yards

15. 24 inches ____ 1 foot   16. 6 yards ____ 24 feet

Lesson 5

Ruler Measurement - Inches

Measure each object to the nearest $\frac{1}{2}$ or $\frac{1}{4}$ inch using the rulers below.

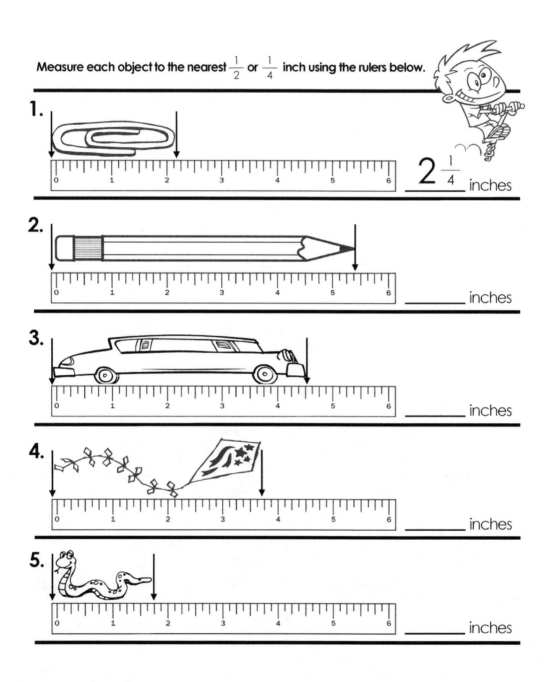

1.

$2\frac{1}{4}$ _____ inches

2.

_____ inches

3.

_____ inches

4.

_____ inches

5.

_____ inches

Ruler Measurement - Centimeters

Measure each object to the nearest centimeter.

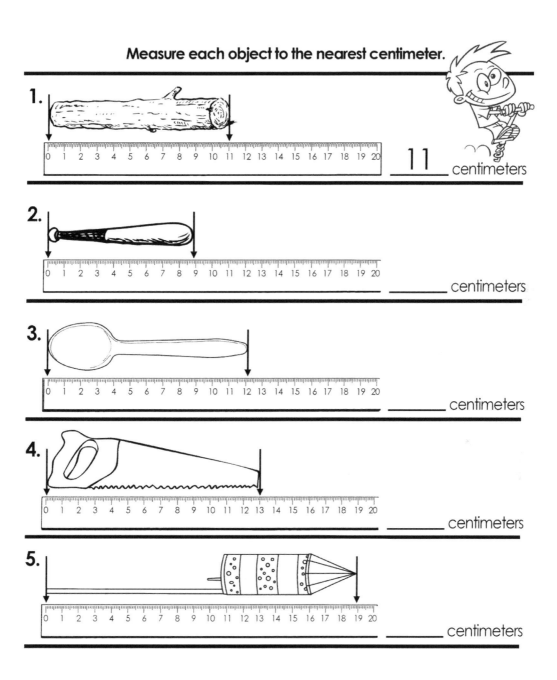

1. _11_ centimeters

2. _____ centimeters

3. _____ centimeters

4. _____ centimeters

5. _____ centimeters

Lesson 6

Liquid Measurement 1

| 2 Cups = 1 Pint | 2 Pints = 1 Quart | 4 Quarts = 1 Gallon |

1 Cup   **1 Pint**   **1 Quart**   **1 Gallon**

Circle the number of objects to match the amount in the box.

1.

2.

3.

4.

5.

Liquid Measurement 2

1 cup (c.) = 8 ounces (oz.)   1 gallon (gal.) = 4 quarts (qt.)
1 pint (pt.) = 2 cups (c.)   1 gallon (gal.) = 8 pints (pt.)
1 quart (qt.) = 2 pints (pt.)   1 gallon (gal.) = 16 cups (c.)
1 quart (qt.) = 4 cups (c.)

Complete the problems below.

1. 14 pt. = ___7___ qt.

2. 3 c. = _____ oz.

3. 2 pt. = _____ c.

4. 16 oz. = _____ c.

5. 2 gal. = _____ c.

6. 2 gal. = _____ pt.

7. 32 c. = _____ gal.

8. 8 pt. = _____ qt.

9. 20 pt. = _____ c.

10. 13 gal. = _____ pt.

11. 10 gal. = _____ pt.

12. 24 oz. = _____ c.

13. 6 gal. = _____ qt.

14. 20 pt. = _____ c.

15. 48 c. = _____ gal.

16. 16 pt. = _____ qt.

17. 5 c. = _____ oz.

18. 6 pt. = _____ c.

19. 48 pt. = _____ gal.

20. 8 pt. = _____ c.

21. 16 pt. = _____ gal.

22. 112 oz. = _____ c.

23. 10 qt. = _____ c.

24. 3 gal. = _____ qt.

Liquid Measurement - Word Problems

Circle the correct answer for each question.

1. Mom is filling up the tub so I can take a bath. How much water does she need?

   20 ounces   ⟨20 gallons⟩

2. Danny's dog is thirsty; how much water should he put in its bowl?

   3 pints   3 gallons   3 ounces

3. The car is low on gasoline. How much gas should we add?

   12 cups   12 gallons   12 pints

4. How much paint should Rhea buy to paint her art project?

   16 ounces   16 quarts   16 gallons

Lesson 1

Explaining Fractions

A **fraction** names a part of a whole. It can also be used to name a part of a group or set.

Fractions are made up of two parts. The **numerator** and the **denominator**.

⬤ ◯ → $\dfrac{1}{4}$ ← The numerator is the number of shaded objects.
◯ ◯ ← The denominator is the total number of objects.

Write what fraction of each set is shaded in.

1. = $\dfrac{1}{3}$ 2. 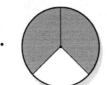 = ☐

3.  = ☐   4.  = ☐

5. = ☐   6.  = ☐

7. = ☐   8.  = ☐

Lesson 2

Comparing Fractions 1

- These fractions have the same denominators.

- We determine which fraction is larger by looking at the numerator.

- 6 is greater than 5. (6 > 5)

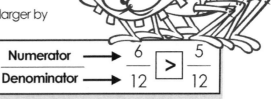

Numerator ⟶ $\dfrac{6}{12}$ > $\dfrac{5}{12}$ ⟵ Denominator

Compare the fractions. Write >, <, or =.

1. $\dfrac{2}{8}$ < $\dfrac{4}{8}$

2. $\dfrac{1}{5}$ ☐ $\dfrac{4}{5}$

3. $\dfrac{8}{10}$ ☐ $\dfrac{6}{10}$

4. $\dfrac{2}{3}$ ☐ $\dfrac{4}{3}$

5. $\dfrac{6}{7}$ ☐ $\dfrac{2}{7}$

6. $\dfrac{10}{15}$ ☐ $\dfrac{2}{15}$

7. $\dfrac{2}{6}$ ☐ $\dfrac{4}{6}$

8. $\dfrac{1}{2}$ ☐ $\dfrac{2}{2}$

9. $\dfrac{5}{10}$ ☐ $\dfrac{3}{10}$

10. $\dfrac{3}{8}$ ☐ $\dfrac{4}{8}$

11. $\dfrac{1}{11}$ ☐ $\dfrac{9}{11}$

12. $\dfrac{3}{5}$ ☐ $\dfrac{1}{5}$

13. $\dfrac{1}{3}$ ☐ $\dfrac{4}{3}$

14. $\dfrac{1}{4}$ ☐ $\dfrac{3}{4}$

15. $\dfrac{7}{9}$ ☐ $\dfrac{5}{9}$

Comparing Fractions 2

Compare the fractions. Write >, <, or =.

1. $\dfrac{3}{9}$ ☐ $\dfrac{4}{9}$

2. $\dfrac{5}{8}$ ☐ $\dfrac{7}{8}$

3. $\dfrac{3}{4}$ ☐ $\dfrac{1}{4}$

4. $\dfrac{1}{2}$ ☐ $\dfrac{2}{2}$

5. $\dfrac{7}{9}$ ☐ $\dfrac{5}{9}$

6. $\dfrac{6}{40}$ ☐ $\dfrac{16}{40}$

7. $\dfrac{10}{13}$ ☐ $\dfrac{12}{13}$

8. $\dfrac{6}{7}$ ☐ $\dfrac{5}{7}$

9. $\dfrac{9}{16}$ ☐ $\dfrac{2}{16}$

10. $\dfrac{10}{11}$ ☐ $\dfrac{2}{11}$

11. $\dfrac{2}{3}$ ☐ $\dfrac{2}{3}$

12. $\dfrac{25}{52}$ ☐ $\dfrac{4}{52}$

13. $\dfrac{60}{78}$ ☐ $\dfrac{9}{78}$

14. $\dfrac{1}{10}$ ☐ $\dfrac{2}{10}$

15. $\dfrac{2}{3}$ ☐ $\dfrac{4}{3}$

16. $\dfrac{1}{12}$ ☐ $\dfrac{2}{12}$

17. $\dfrac{1}{9}$ ☐ $\dfrac{2}{9}$

18. $\dfrac{23}{29}$ ☐ $\dfrac{4}{29}$

19. $\dfrac{4}{7}$ ☐ $\dfrac{6}{7}$

20. $\dfrac{111}{12}$ ☐ $\dfrac{12}{12}$

Lesson 3

Ordering Fractions

Write these fractions in order from least to greatest.

1. $1\frac{6}{10},\ 2\frac{3}{10},\ 1\frac{1}{10},\ 2\frac{1}{10}$ $1\frac{1}{10},\ 1\frac{6}{10},\ 2\frac{1}{10},\ 2\frac{3}{10}$

2. $4\frac{4}{8},\ 9\frac{6}{8},\ 6\frac{2}{8},\ 9\frac{3}{8}$

3. $6\frac{1}{4},\ 7\frac{1}{4},\ 6\frac{2}{4},\ 7\frac{3}{4}$

4. $8\frac{1}{9},\ 9\frac{1}{9},\ 8\frac{2}{9},\ 8\frac{3}{9}$

5. $3\frac{8}{12},\ 3\frac{1}{12},\ 1\frac{1}{12},\ 2\frac{3}{12}$

6. $5\frac{3}{54},\ 5\frac{2}{54},\ 5\frac{1}{54},\ 5\frac{7}{54}$

Lesson 4

Adding Fractions with Common Denominators 1

To add fractions with common denominators, just add the numerators. The denominators will remain the same.

$$\text{Numerators} \longrightarrow \qquad \frac{2}{9} + \frac{3}{9} = \frac{2+3}{9} = \frac{5}{9}$$
$$\text{Common Denominators} \longrightarrow$$

Add the fractions below.

1. $\dfrac{1}{5} + \dfrac{3}{5} = \dfrac{4}{5}$

2. $\dfrac{5}{10} + \dfrac{3}{10} = \underline{\quad}$

3. $\dfrac{3}{6} + \dfrac{2}{6} = \underline{\quad}$

4. $\dfrac{7}{12} + \dfrac{3}{12} = \underline{\quad}$

5. $\dfrac{4}{9} + \dfrac{4}{9} = \underline{\quad}$

6. $\dfrac{6}{14} + \dfrac{2}{14} = \underline{\quad}$

7. $\dfrac{3}{7} + \dfrac{2}{7} = \underline{\quad}$

8. $\dfrac{1}{4} + \dfrac{2}{4} = \underline{\quad}$

9. $\dfrac{2}{6} + \dfrac{3}{6} = \underline{\quad}$

10. $\dfrac{4}{8} + \dfrac{3}{8} = \underline{\quad}$

11. $\dfrac{6}{11} + \dfrac{3}{11} = \underline{\quad}$

12. $\dfrac{7}{15} + \dfrac{5}{15} = \underline{\quad}$

13. $\dfrac{3}{14} + \dfrac{9}{14} = \underline{\quad}$

14. $\dfrac{1}{3} + \dfrac{1}{3} = \underline{\quad}$

15. $\dfrac{2}{8} + \dfrac{4}{8} = \underline{\quad}$

16. $\dfrac{3}{5} + \dfrac{1}{5} = \underline{\quad}$

17. $\dfrac{9}{13} + \dfrac{2}{13} = \underline{\quad}$

18. $\dfrac{1}{10} + \dfrac{6}{10} = \underline{\quad}$

Adding Fractions with Common Denominators 2

To add fractions with common denominators, just add the numerators. The denominators will remain the same.

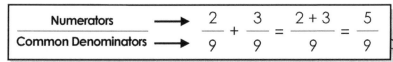

Numerators ⟶

Common Denominators ⟶

$$\frac{2}{9} + \frac{3}{9} = \frac{2+3}{9} = \frac{5}{9}$$

Add the fractions below.

1. $\dfrac{2}{5} + \dfrac{1}{5} + \dfrac{1}{5} =$ _____

2. $\dfrac{15}{59} + \dfrac{3}{59} + \dfrac{9}{59} =$ _____

3. $\dfrac{4}{7} + \dfrac{1}{7} + \dfrac{2}{7} =$ _____

4. $\dfrac{6}{13} + \dfrac{2}{13} + \dfrac{1}{13} =$ _____

5. $\dfrac{4}{15} + \dfrac{4}{15} + \dfrac{3}{15} =$ _____

6. $\dfrac{44}{209} + \dfrac{19}{209} + \dfrac{7}{209} =$ _____

7. $\dfrac{6}{22} + \dfrac{1}{22} + \dfrac{9}{22} =$ _____

8. $\dfrac{4}{33} + \dfrac{1}{33} + \dfrac{16}{33} =$ _____

9. $\dfrac{3}{45} + \dfrac{10}{45} + \dfrac{11}{45} =$ _____

10. $\dfrac{63}{138} + \dfrac{23}{138} + \dfrac{18}{138} =$ _____

11. $\dfrac{1}{6} + \dfrac{2}{6} + \dfrac{1}{6} =$ _____

12. $\dfrac{3}{10} + \dfrac{3}{10} + \dfrac{1}{10} =$ _____

Lesson 5

Subtracting Fractions with Common Denominators 1

To subtract fractions with common denominators, just subtract the numerators. The denominators will remain the same.

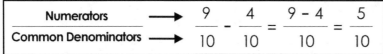

Numerators $\longrightarrow$ $\dfrac{9}{10} - \dfrac{4}{10} = \dfrac{9-4}{10} = \dfrac{5}{10}$
Common Denominators $\longrightarrow$

Subtract the fractions below.

---

1. $\dfrac{7}{15} - \dfrac{3}{15} = \dfrac{4}{15}$

2. $\dfrac{7}{9} - \dfrac{2}{9} = $ ____

3. $\dfrac{12}{14} - \dfrac{7}{14} = $ ____

4. $\dfrac{8}{8} - \dfrac{6}{8} = $ ____

5. $\dfrac{28}{39} - \dfrac{19}{39} = $ ____

6. $\dfrac{24}{39} - \dfrac{11}{39} = $ ____

7. $\dfrac{9}{10} - \dfrac{2}{10} = $ ____

8. $\dfrac{13}{15} - \dfrac{9}{15} = $ ____

9. $\dfrac{13}{16} - \dfrac{3}{16} = $ ____

10. $\dfrac{6}{7} - \dfrac{4}{7} = $ ____

11. $\dfrac{10}{26} - \dfrac{8}{26} = $ ____

12. $\dfrac{60}{62} - \dfrac{41}{62} = $ ____

13. $\dfrac{19}{24} - \dfrac{10}{24} = $ ____

14. $\dfrac{46}{54} - \dfrac{17}{54} = $ ____

15. $\dfrac{98}{98} - \dfrac{15}{98} = $ ____

Subtracting Fractions with Common Denominators 2

To subtract fractions with common denominators, just subtract the numerators. The denominators will remain the same.

Numerators $\longrightarrow$ $\dfrac{9}{10} - \dfrac{4}{10} = \dfrac{9-4}{10} = \dfrac{5}{10}$

Common Denominators $\longrightarrow$

Subtract the fractions below.

---

1. $\dfrac{23}{44} - \dfrac{9}{44} =$ _____

2. $\dfrac{6}{10} - \dfrac{4}{10} =$ _____

3. $\dfrac{30}{63} - \dfrac{19}{63} =$ _____

4. $\dfrac{45}{90} - \dfrac{42}{90} =$ _____

5. $\dfrac{12}{12} - \dfrac{6}{12} =$ _____

6. $\dfrac{28}{30} - \dfrac{8}{30} =$ _____

7. $\dfrac{4}{7} - \dfrac{1}{7} =$ _____

8. $\dfrac{15}{24} - \dfrac{6}{24} =$ _____

9. $\dfrac{45}{98} - \dfrac{31}{98} =$ _____

10. $\dfrac{5}{10} - \dfrac{2}{10} =$ _____

11. $\dfrac{5}{15} - \dfrac{3}{15} =$ _____

12. $\dfrac{8}{12} - \dfrac{3}{12} =$ _____

13. $\dfrac{20}{34} - \dfrac{19}{34} =$ _____

14. $\dfrac{6}{8} - \dfrac{3}{8} =$ _____

15. $\dfrac{14}{23} - \dfrac{7}{23} =$ _____

Lesson 6

Adding Mixed Numbers with Common Denominators

A **mixed number** is a number written as a whole number and a fraction.

When adding mixed numbers with common denominators, add the whole numbers first, then add the numerators. The denominators will remain the same.

$$1\frac{2}{4} + 5\frac{1}{4} = 6\frac{3}{4} \longleftarrow \frac{\text{Numerator}}{\text{Denominator}}$$

Add the mixed numbers below.

1. $5\frac{3}{8}$
    $+3\frac{2}{8}$
    _____
    $8\frac{5}{8}$

2. $2\frac{2}{5}$
    $+1\frac{2}{5}$
    _____

3. $9\frac{3}{10}$
    $+3\frac{4}{10}$
    _____

4. $2\frac{6}{15}$
    $+2\frac{4}{15}$
    _____

5. $4\frac{9}{21}$
    $+5\frac{5}{21}$
    _____

6. $7\frac{20}{42}$
    $+6\frac{14}{42}$
    _____

7. $13\frac{7}{9}$
    $+3\frac{1}{9}$
    _____

8. $12\frac{6}{29}$
    $+11\frac{9}{29}$
    _____

Lesson 7

Subtracting Mixed Numbers with Common Denominators

A **mixed number** is a number written as a whole number and a fraction.

When subtracting mixed numbers with common denominators, subtract the whole numbers first, then subtract the numerators. The denominators will remain the same.

$$9\frac{5}{6} - 4\frac{2}{6} = 5\frac{3}{6}$$ ⟵ Numerator
⟵ Denominator

Subtract the mixed numbers below.

1. $6\frac{3}{4}$
  $- 4\frac{1}{4}$
  $2\frac{2}{4}$

2. $8\frac{4}{6}$
  $- 3\frac{2}{6}$

3. $5\frac{8}{9}$
  $- 2\frac{7}{9}$

4. $9\frac{11}{13}$
  $- 8\frac{9}{13}$

5. $32\frac{15}{21}$
  $-18\frac{5}{21}$

6. $12\frac{7}{30}$
  $- 2\frac{2}{30}$

7. $17\frac{20}{26}$
  $-11\frac{12}{26}$

8. $25\frac{13}{17}$
  $-18\frac{8}{17}$

Lesson 8

Reducing Fractions 1

- Reducing (or simplifying) fractions means reducing a fraction to the lowest possible terms.
  - To do this, find a number that both the numerator and the denominator of the fraction are divisible by. Use that number as the numerator and denominator of a new fraction equal to one. Then divide the fractions.

Example 1:	Example 2:
$\dfrac{15}{20} \div \dfrac{5}{5} = \dfrac{3}{4}$	$\dfrac{3}{9} \div \dfrac{3}{3} = \dfrac{1}{3}$
$\dfrac{15}{20} = \left\lceil \dfrac{3}{4} \right\rceil$	$\dfrac{3}{9} = \left\lceil \dfrac{1}{3} \right\rceil$

Write the problems out and reduce the fractions below.

1. $\dfrac{5}{15} \div \dfrac{3}{3} = \dfrac{1}{3}$

2. $\dfrac{4}{12} \div \underline{\quad} = \underline{\quad}$

3. $\dfrac{6}{15} \div \underline{\quad} = \underline{\quad}$

4. $\dfrac{8}{10} \div \underline{\quad} = \underline{\quad}$

5. $\dfrac{10}{25} \div \underline{\quad} = \underline{\quad}$

6. $\dfrac{20}{25} \div \underline{\quad} = \underline{\quad}$

Reducing Fractions 2

- Reducing (or simplifying) fractions means reducing a fraction to the lowest possible terms.
    - To do this, find a number that both the numerator and the denominator of the fraction are divisible by. Use that number as the numerator and denominator of a new fraction equal to one. Then divide the fractions.

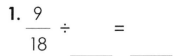

Write the problems out and reduce the fractions below.

1. $\dfrac{9}{18} \div \underline{\hspace{1cm}} = \underline{\hspace{1cm}}$

2. $\dfrac{6}{28} \div \underline{\hspace{1cm}} = \underline{\hspace{1cm}}$

3. $\dfrac{15}{18} \div \underline{\hspace{1cm}} = \underline{\hspace{1cm}}$

4. $\dfrac{12}{16} \div \underline{\hspace{1cm}} = \underline{\hspace{1cm}}$

5. $\dfrac{18}{36} \div \underline{\hspace{1cm}} = \underline{\hspace{1cm}}$

6. $\dfrac{24}{75} \div \underline{\hspace{1cm}} = \underline{\hspace{1cm}}$

7. $\dfrac{7}{49} \div \underline{\hspace{1cm}} = \underline{\hspace{1cm}}$

8. $\dfrac{27}{81} \div \underline{\hspace{1cm}} = \underline{\hspace{1cm}}$

Practice Test #1

Practice Questions

1. Donald has the amount of money shown below. How much money does he have?

Ⓐ $6.14

Ⓑ $6.19

Ⓒ $6.24

Ⓓ $6.29

2. Which fraction is represented by the diagram shown below?

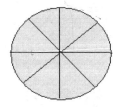 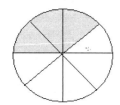

Ⓐ $1\frac{1}{8}$

Ⓑ $1\frac{1}{4}$

Ⓒ $1\frac{3}{8}$

Ⓓ $1\frac{1}{2}$

3. Which of the following models represents a fraction equivalent to $\frac{2}{5}$?

Ⓐ

Ⓑ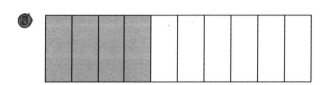

Ⓒ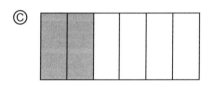

Ⓓ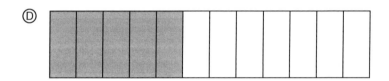

4. If Hannah drives 1104 miles a month and Carrie drives 1339 miles a month. How many miles do they drive each month combined?

_____ 2443miles _____

5. Jasper collects 1,082 cans of food. He gives a certain number of cans to the first local charity he finds. He now has 602 cans of food. How many cans of food did he give to the first local charity?

Ⓐ 430

Ⓑ 480

Ⓒ 682

Ⓓ 1,684

6. Which of the following models represents a fraction less than the fraction shown below?

$\frac{2}{9}$

Ⓐ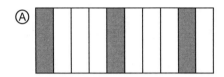

Ⓑ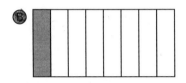

Ⓒ

Ⓓ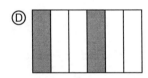

7. Amanda creates the base of a picture frame, using 4.55 inches of red fabric and 6.25 inches of blue fabric. How many inches of fabric are used to create the base of the frame?

Ⓐ 10.80 inches

Ⓑ 10.85 inches

Ⓒ 10.75 inches

Ⓓ 10.90 inches

8. Travis has a stick that is 5/16 of a meter long, and Steven has a stick that is 7/8 of a meter long. If they lay the sticks end to end how long would they be?

Ⓐ $\frac{12}{16}$ meter

Ⓑ $1\frac{3}{16}$

Ⓒ $1\frac{3}{8}$

Ⓓ $1\frac{1}{8}$

9. Which of the following number sentences is represented by the array shown below?

X X X X X X
X X X X X X
X X X X X X
X X X X X X

Ⓐ $4 + 6 = 10$

Ⓑ $4 \times 6 = 24$

Ⓒ $24 - 6 = 18$

Ⓓ $24 \div 3 = 8$

10. Which of the following number sentences is represented by the model shown below?

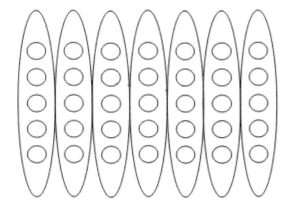

Ⓐ $7 \times 7 = 49$

Ⓑ $35 - 7 = 28$

Ⓒ $7 + 5 = 12$

⬤ $35 \div 7 = 5$

11. Hannah ran 12 laps every day for 8 days. How many laps did she run in all?

Ⓐ 108

⬤ 96

Ⓒ 84

Ⓓ 72

12. Kevin approved 13 trees out of every group of trees he surveyed. He surveyed 15 groups of trees. How many trees did he approve?

Ⓐ 155

Ⓑ 165

⬤ 195

Ⓓ 205

13. Monique has $690 to spend on a 3-day trip. She plans to spend an equal amount of money per day. How many dollars can she spend per day?

230 money

14. Three friends sold cupcakes for a fundraiser. Eli sold 84 cupcakes, John sold 46 cupcakes, and Kim sold 72 cupcakes. Which of the following is the best estimate for the number of cupcakes the three friends sold in all?

Ⓐ 180

Ⓑ 200

Ⓒ 210

Ⓓ 190

15. Lynn has $316 to spend on groceries for the month. He plans to spend the same amount of money on groceries each week. Which of the following is the best <u>estimate</u> for the amount of money he can spend on groceries each week?

Ⓐ $65

Ⓑ $75

Ⓒ $90

Ⓓ $95

16. Carlisle charges $21.95 per hair cut and has completed 30 haircuts this week. Which of the following is the best approximation for the total charges for all haircuts?

Ⓐ $450

Ⓑ $600

Ⓒ $750

Ⓓ $800

17. Which of the following number sentences belongs in the fact family shown below?

$$7 \times 6 = 42$$
$$6 \times 7 = 42$$
$$42 \div 7 = 6$$

Ⓐ $7 + 6 = 13$

Ⓑ $42 \div 6 = 7$

Ⓒ $42 + 7 = 49$

Ⓓ $42 - 6 = 36$

18. Billy is going on vacation. He will travel a total of 1486 miles while he is gone. If Location A is 572 miles away from home and then Location B is 437 miles from location A. How long is the trip from Location B back to home?

_____

19. A door is $7\frac{1}{4}$ feet tall. How many inches is it?

75 in.

_____

20. Mrs. Thompson writes the number sentences shown below:

$$100 \times 13 = 1300$$
$$100 \times 14 = 1400$$
$$100 \times 15 = 1500$$
$$100 \times 24 = ?$$

What is the product of the last number sentence?

Ⓐ 2200

Ⓑ 2300

◉ 2400

Ⓓ 2500

21. The number of sit-ups Aisha has completed over a period of 3 days is shown in the table below.

Day	Number of Sit-ups
1	35
2	70
3	105

4 | 140
5 | 175
6 | 210
7 | 245

If this pattern continues, how many sit-ups will she have completed after 7 days?

245

- 131 -

22. Which of the following correctly describes the relationship between the values of x and y, as shown in the table below?

x	y
1	4
2	8
3	12
4	16

Ⓐ The value of *x* is 6 less than the value of *y*

Ⓑ The value of *y* is 4 times the value of *x*

Ⓒ The value of *y* is 4 more than the value of *x*

Ⓓ The value of *x* is 1 less than the value of *y*

23. If the measure of angle *BAC* is 38° and the measure of angle *DAE* is 49°, then what is the measure of angle *CAD*?

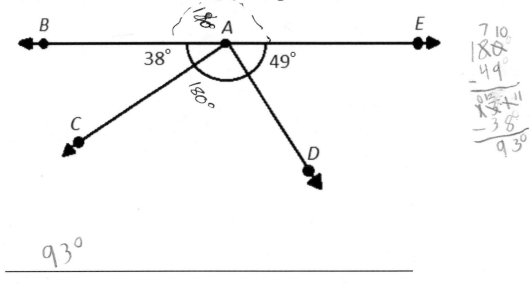

93°

_____

24. A farm has only cows and chickens. There are 5 chicken coops with 14 chickens each, and 6 barns with 16 cows each. How many total animals are on the farm?

Ⓐ 41

Ⓑ 330

Ⓒ 164

Ⓓ 166

$$\begin{array}{r} \overset{2}{14} \\ \times\ 5 \\ \hline 70 \end{array} \qquad \begin{array}{r} \overset{3}{16} \\ \times\ 6 \\ \hline 96 \end{array} \qquad \begin{array}{r} 70 \\ +\ 96 \\ \hline 166 \end{array}$$

25. Which shape has 5 sides?

Ⓐ hexagon

Ⓑ pentagon

Ⓒ octagon

Ⓓ heptagon

26. Given the numbers below, fill in the blank with the correct symbol (<, >, =) to make the statement true.

4.22 __>__ 4.2

.09 __<__ .9

2.72 __>__ 2.702

27. Which of the following equation equals $4 \times \frac{4}{5}$?

Ⓐ $8 \times \frac{1}{5}$

Ⓑ $4 \times \frac{3}{5}$

Ⓒ $5 \times \frac{4}{5}$

Ⓓ $16 \times \frac{1}{5}$

28. The shape below represents a reflection about the axis. Which of the following statements is true?

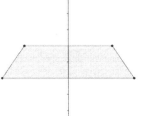

Ⓐ The shape has one line of symmetry

Ⓑ The shape has two lines of symmetry

Ⓒ The shape has four lines of symmetry

Ⓓ The shape does not have any lines of symmetry

29. What number is represented by Point A, shown on the number line below?

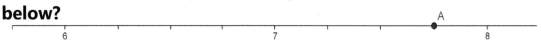

Ⓐ $7\frac{3}{8}$

Ⓑ $7\frac{1}{2}$

Ⓒ $7\frac{1}{4}$

Ⓓ $7\frac{3}{4}$

30. Which point, on the number line below, represents $14\frac{2}{10}$?

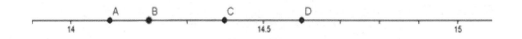

Ⓐ Point A

Ⓑ Point B

Ⓒ Point C

Ⓓ Point D

31. Which of the following are multiples of 7? Select all that apply.

- (I.) 7
- (II.) 21
- III. 27
- IV. 39
- (V.) 42
- (VI.) 77

32. Jason walks 2,847 feet to school. Kevin walks 3,128 feet to school. What is the difference in the distance that they walk to school?

281
_____

33. Ana draws a line with chalk that is $14\frac{5}{8}$ feet long. Then she erases $3\frac{3}{8}$ feet. How long is the line now?

$11\frac{2}{8}$
_____

34. Which of the following are factors of 42? Select all that apply.

- (I.) 1 and 42
- II. 2 and 22
- (III.) 3 and 14
- IV. 4 and 11
- V. 5 and 8
- (VI.) 6 and 7

35. A box has a length of 7.5 inches, a width of 3.85 inches, and a height of 2.3 inches. Which of the following best represents the volume of the box?

Ⓐ 28 in³

Ⓑ 36 in³

Ⓒ 48 in³

Ⓓ 64 in³

36. Sally is making cupcakes. She needs $\frac{1}{4}$ cup of sugar for every 3 cupcakes. How many cups does she need for 24 cupcakes?

Ⓐ $1\frac{1}{2}$ cups

Ⓑ 8 cups

Ⓒ $\frac{3}{4}$ cup

Ⓓ 2 cups

37. Aubrey arrived at the party at the time shown on the clock below. It is now four-thirty. How much time has passed since she arrived at the party?

$$2{:}15$$

Ⓐ 1 hour, 45 minutes

Ⓑ 2 hours, 5 minutes

Ⓒ 2 hours, 15 minutes

Ⓓ 2 hours, 30 minutes

38. The bar graph below represents student preferences for different parks in Flagstaff, Arizona.

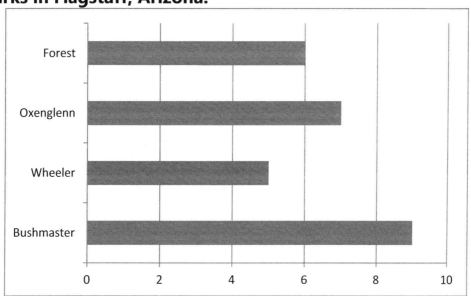

Which park is preferred by the most students?

Ⓐ Bushmaster

Ⓑ Wheeler

Ⓒ Oxenglenn

Ⓓ Forest

39. A cafeteria offers 3 meats, 3 vegetables, 2 breads, and 2 desserts. How many possible meal combinations are there?

3m , 2b ,

40. The average number of miles per hour driven by a sample of drivers is shown below.

65, 70, 60, 55, 70, 65, 70, 60, 65, 70, 55, 65, 70, 55, 60

Based on the data, which average speed is driven by the most drivers?

Ⓐ 55

Ⓑ 60

Ⓒ 65

Ⓓ 70

Practice Test #2

Practice Questions

1. A room has 6 rows of 9 chairs. The room next to it has 32 chairs. Together how many chairs do they have?

    Ⓐ 54

    Ⓑ 56

    ● 86

    Ⓓ 84

2. Amanda buys a sandwich and pays the amount of money shown below. How much does she pay?

    Ⓐ $3.56

    Ⓑ $3.61

    Ⓒ $3.50

    Ⓓ $3.51

3. Which of the following sets represents a fraction equivalent to $\frac{8}{12}$?

Ⓐ

Ⓑ  $\frac{2 \times 4 = 8}{3 \times 4 = 12}$

Ⓒ

Ⓓ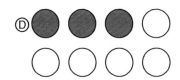

4. Which fraction is represented by the diagram shown below?

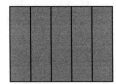 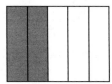

Ⓐ $1\frac{1}{2}$

Ⓑ $1\frac{2}{5}$

Ⓒ $1\frac{3}{5}$

Ⓓ $1\frac{3}{4}$

5. Which of the following models represents a fraction equal to the fraction shown below?

$$\frac{5}{15}$$

(A)

(B)

(C)

(D)

6. Which of the following fractions are equal to $\frac{2}{3}$? Select all that apply.

I. $\frac{1}{6}$

II. $\frac{6}{9}$

III. $\frac{4}{6}$

IV. $\frac{5}{8}$

V. $\frac{6}{10}$

7. Martin saved $156 in September, $173 in October, and $219 in November. How much money did he save during the three months?

Ⓐ $538

Ⓑ $569

Ⓒ $548

Ⓓ $576

8. Andrea pays $120 more in rent per month this year than she did last year. She pays $763 per month this year. How much did she pay per month last year?

Ⓐ $663

Ⓑ $643

Ⓒ $863

Ⓓ $883

9. Which sum is represented by the diagram shown below?

 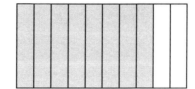

Ⓐ 1.08

Ⓑ 1.09

Ⓒ 1.10

Ⓓ 1.11

10. Which fact is represented by the array shown below?

Ⓐ $3 + 7 = 10$

Ⓑ $21 - 7 = 14$

Ⓒ $3 \times 7 = 21$

Ⓓ $10 + 7 = 17$

11. Eli has 42 crayons and plans to give the same number of crayons to each of his 6 friends. Which number sentence can be used to find the number of crayons he will give to each friend?

Ⓐ $42 - 6 = 36$

Ⓑ $42 \div 6 = 7$

Ⓒ $42 \times 6 = 252$

Ⓓ $42 + 6 = 48$

12. Alex buys 3 gallons of milk each week. How many gallons of milk does he buy in 12 weeks?

Ⓐ 18

Ⓑ 24

Ⓒ 36

Ⓓ 48

13. A candle-making shop sold 18 candles on Friday, 37 candles on Saturday, and 23 candles on Sunday. Which of the following is the best estimate for the number of candles sold during the three days?

Ⓐ 60

Ⓑ 70

Ⓒ 80

Ⓓ 90

14. Isabelle must drive 1,482 miles. She plans to drive approximately the same number of miles per day over the period of 5 days. Which of the following is the best approximation for the number of miles she will drive per day?

Ⓐ 250

Ⓑ 300

Ⓒ 350

Ⓓ 400

15. A consultant earned $17,850 over the course of 6 months. Which of the following is the best approximation for the amount of money the consultant earned each month?

Ⓐ $2,500

Ⓑ $3,000

Ⓒ $3,500

Ⓓ $4,000

16. Mr. Jacobsen buys 32 boxes of oatmeal. Each box contains 20 packets of oatmeal. How many total packets of oatmeal did he buy?

_____

17. Mr. Johnson ordered 1 pizza for every 3 kids in his class. If he ordered 7 pizzas then how many kids does he have in his class?

_____

18. Part A: What fraction does the shaded area of the cirle below represent?

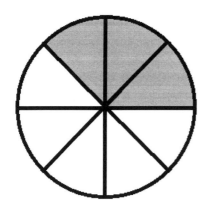

(A) $\frac{2}{3}$

(B) $\frac{3}{6}$

(C) $\frac{3}{8}$

(D) $\frac{1}{3}$

Part B: If 3 more slices of the circle are shaded in then what fraction would it be?

Ⓐ $\frac{5}{8}$

Ⓑ $\frac{5}{6}$

Ⓒ $\frac{2}{3}$

Ⓓ $\frac{3}{4}$

19. The number of miles Brad has driven over a period of 3 days is shown in the table below.

Day	Number of Miles
1	275
2	550
3	825

If this pattern continues, how many miles will he have driven after 8 days?

Ⓐ 2,000

Ⓑ 2,025

Ⓒ 2,075

Ⓓ 2,200

20. Andrew displays the following sets of data to his colleagues. Which of the following represents the relationship between the first and second columns of data?

4	16
7	19
12	24
14	26
19	31

Ⓐ The values in the second column are 12 more than the values in the first column.

Ⓑ The values in the first column are one-fourth of the values in the second column.

Ⓒ The values in the first column are 11 fewer than the values in the second column.

Ⓓ The values in the second column are 3 more than the values in the first column.

21. Jenny will be in a parade and will be throwing out candy. She has 20 pieces of candy, but she thinks that she will need 12 times that much since the parade is so long. How many pieces does she think she needs?

_____

22. Morris needs to define an obtuse angle. Which of the following correctly describes the requirements for such an angle?

Ⓐ An angle with a measure greater than 180 degrees

Ⓑ An angle with a measure greater than 120 degrees

Ⓒ An angle with a measure less than 90 degrees

Ⓓ An angle with a measure greater than 90 degrees

23. If John works 386 minutes a day, how many minutes does he work in a 5 day work week?

_____

24. Which of the following angles is acute?

Ⓐ

Ⓑ

Ⓒ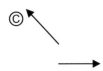

Ⓓ

25. Sally eats $\frac{1}{4}$ of a pie, Jesse eats $\frac{1}{8}$ of the same pie, and Lisa eats $\frac{3}{8}$ of the pie. How much of the pie is left?

Ⓐ $\frac{1}{4}$

Ⓑ $\frac{3}{8}$

Ⓒ $\frac{1}{8}$

Ⓓ $\frac{1}{2}$

26. Part A: Which of the following figures does not have any parallel sides?

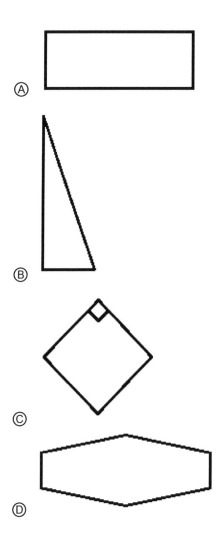

Ⓐ

Ⓑ

Ⓒ

Ⓓ

Part B: Which one does not have any perpendicular sides?

Ⓐ Figure A

Ⓑ Figure B

Ⓒ Figure C

Ⓓ Figure D

27. What decimal is represented by Point P, shown on the number line below?

Ⓐ 5.6

Ⓑ 5.7

Ⓒ 5.8

Ⓓ 5.9

28. What Point represents $3\frac{3}{4}$, on the number line below?

Ⓐ Point A

Ⓑ Point B

Ⓒ Point C

Ⓓ Point D

29. A school has 14 classrooms. Each classroom has 22 students in it. How many total students are in the school?

Ⓐ 36

Ⓑ 288

Ⓒ 304

Ⓓ 308

30. Part A: A teacher took a survey of 4th, 5th, and 6th grade students about their favorite animals. Based on the results below how many total students were surveyed?

	Cat	Dog	Fish	Bird
4th Grade	8	10	5	4
5th Grade	10	12	4	4
6th Grade	7	13	2	3

_____

Part B: What fraction of 5th grade students chose cats as their favorite animal?

Ⓐ $\frac{2}{3}$

Ⓑ $\frac{1}{3}$

Ⓒ $\frac{12}{30}$

Ⓓ $\frac{10}{28}$

31. Given the number 2,573. The number 5 is in what place?

Ⓐ ones

Ⓑ tens

Ⓒ hundreds

Ⓓ thousands

32. In the rectangle below each small square is one square unit. How many square units make up the area of the entire rectangle?

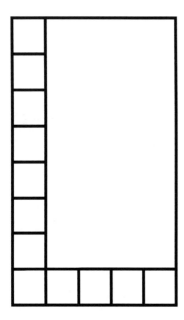

   Ⓐ 28

   Ⓑ 40

   Ⓒ 12

   Ⓓ 35

33. Hannah weighs approximately 27 pounds. What is her approximate weight, in ounces?

   Ⓐ 432 ounces

   Ⓑ 378 ounces

   Ⓒ 324 ounces

   Ⓓ 438 ounces

34. Jamal drinks 2 quarts of water per day. How many cups of water does he drink?

35. If Kara has 24 hair pins and she buys 6 more packages that each contain 12 hair pins. How many hair pins does she have now?

_____

36. Jim drives 1920 miles. He used 6 tanks of gas to drive that far. How many miles can he go on one tank of gas?

_____

37. Andy surveys his classmates to determine their favorite season of the year. The results are shown in the table below.

Season	Number of Students
Fall	7
Winter	3
Spring	12
Summer	18

Which circle graph correctly represents the results?

Ⓐ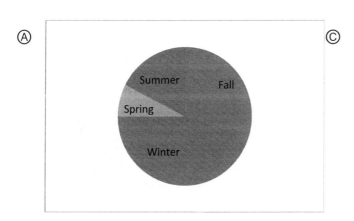

©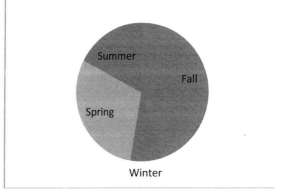

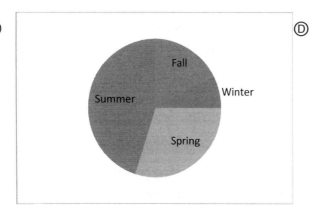

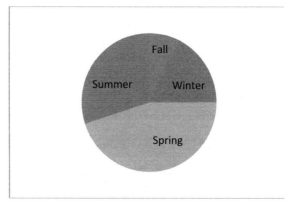

38. The bar graph below represents teacher preferences for different vacation states.

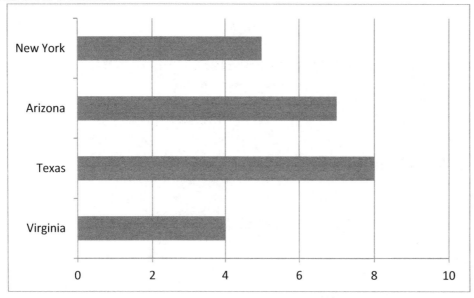

Which state was preferred by the fewest number of teachers?

Ⓐ Virginia

Ⓑ Arizona

Ⓒ Texas

Ⓓ New York

39. Alana can choose from 2 shirts, 2 pairs of jeans, 3 pairs of socks, and 2 pairs of shoes. How many possible outfit combinations can she make?

_____

40. The scores on Mrs. Rodriguez's math test are shown below.

95, 78, 92, 99, 74, 83, 89, 92, 79, 85, 87, 90, 88, 92, 79

Which test score was received by the most students?

Ⓐ 78

Ⓑ 90

Ⓒ 92

Ⓓ 79

Success Strategies

The most important thing you can do is to ignore your fears and jump into the test immediately. Do not be overwhelmed by any strange-sounding terms. You have to jump into the test like jumping into a pool—all at once is the easiest way.

Make Predictions

As you read and understand the question, try to guess what the answer will be. Remember that several of the answer choices are wrong, and once you begin reading them, your mind will immediately become cluttered with answer choices designed to throw you off. Your mind is typically the most focused immediately after you have read the question and digested its contents. If you can, try to predict what the correct answer will be. You may be surprised at what you can predict.

Quickly scan the choices and see if your prediction is in the listed answer choices. If it is, then you can be quite confident that you have the right answer. It still won't hurt to check the other answer choices, but most of the time, you've got it!

Answer the Question

It may seem obvious to only pick answer choices that answer the question, but the test writers can create some excellent answer choices that are wrong. Don't pick an answer just because it sounds right, or you believe it to be true. It MUST answer the question. Once you've made your selection, always go back and check it against the question and make sure that you didn't misread the question and that the answer choice does answer the question posed.

Benchmark

After you read the first answer choice, decide if you think it sounds correct or not. If it doesn't, move on to the next answer choice. If it does, mentally mark that answer choice. This doesn't mean that you've definitely selected it as your answer choice, it just means that it's the best you've seen thus far.

Go ahead and read the next choice. If the next choice is worse than the one you've already selected, keep going to the next answer choice. If the next choice is better than the choice you've already selected, mentally mark the new answer choice as your best guess.

The first answer choice that you select becomes your standard. Every other answer choice must be benchmarked against that standard. That choice is correct until proven otherwise by another answer choice beating it out. Once you've decided that no other answer choice seems as good, do one final check to ensure that your answer choice answers the question posed.

Valid Information

Don't discount any of the information provided in the question. Every piece of information may be necessary to determine the correct answer. None of the information in the question is there to throw you off (while the answer choices will certainly have information to throw you off). If two seemingly unrelated topics are discussed, don't ignore either. You can be confident there is a relationship, or it wouldn't be included in the question, and you are probably going to have to determine what is that relationship to find the answer.

Avoid "Fact Traps"

Don't get distracted by a choice that is factually true. Your search is for the answer that answers the question. Stay focused and don't fall for an answer that is true but irrelevant. Always go back to the question and make sure you're choosing an answer that actually answers the question and is not just a true statement. An answer can be factually correct, but it MUST answer the question asked. Additionally, two answers can both be seemingly correct, so be sure to read all of the answer choices, and make sure that you get the one that BEST answers the question.

Milk the Question

Some of the questions may throw you completely off. They might deal with a subject you have not been exposed to, or one that you haven't reviewed in years. While your lack of knowledge about the subject will be a hindrance, the question itself can give you many clues that will help you find the correct answer. Read the question carefully and look for clues. Watch particularly for adjectives and nouns describing difficult terms or words that you don't recognize. Regardless of whether you completely understand a word or not, replacing it with a synonym, either provided or one you more familiar with, may help you to understand what the questions are asking. Rather than wracking your mind about specific detailed information concerning a difficult term or word, try to use mental substitutes that are easier to understand.

The Trap of Familiarity

Don't just choose a word because you recognize it. On difficult questions, you may not recognize a number of words in the answer choices. The test writers don't put "make-believe" words on the test, so don't think that just because you only recognize all the words in one answer choice that that answer choice must be correct. If you only recognize words in one answer choice, then focus on that one. Is it correct? Try your best to determine if it is correct. If it is, that's great. If not, eliminate it. Each word and answer choice you eliminate increases your chances of getting the question correct, even if you then have to guess among the unfamiliar choices.

Eliminate Answers

Eliminate choices as soon as you realize they are wrong. But be careful! Make sure you consider all of the possible answer choices. Just because one appears right, doesn't mean that the next one won't be even better! The test writers will usually put more than one good answer choice for every question, so read all of them. Don't worry if you are stuck between two that seem right. By getting down to just two remaining possible choices, your odds are now 50/50. Rather than wasting too much time, play the odds. You are guessing, but guessing wisely because you've been able to knock out some of the answer choices that you know are wrong. If you are eliminating choices and realize that the last answer choice you are left with is also obviously wrong, don't panic. Start over and consider each choice again. There may easily be something that you missed the first time and will realize on the second pass.

Tough Questions

If you are stumped on a problem or it appears too hard or too difficult, don't waste time. Move on! Remember though, if you can quickly check for obviously incorrect answer choices, your chances of guessing correctly are greatly improved. Before you completely give up, at least try to knock out a couple of possible answers. Eliminate what you can and then guess at the remaining answer choices before moving on.

Brainstorm

If you get stuck on a difficult question, spend a few seconds quickly brainstorming. Run through the complete list of possible answer choices. Look at each choice and ask yourself, "Could this answer the question satisfactorily?" Go through each answer choice and consider it independently of the others. By systematically going through all possibilities, you may find something that you would otherwise overlook. Remember though that when you get stuck, it's important to try to keep moving.

Read Carefully

Understand the problem. Read the question and answer choices carefully. Don't miss the question because you misread the terms. You have plenty of time to read each question thoroughly and make sure you understand what is being asked. Yet a happy medium must be attained, so don't waste too much time. You must read carefully, but efficiently.

Face Value

When in doubt, use common sense. Always accept the situation in the problem at face value. Don't read too much into it. These problems will not require you to make huge leaps of logic. The test writers aren't trying to throw you off with a cheap trick. If you have to go beyond creativity and make a leap of logic in order to have an answer choice answer the question, then you should look at the other answer choices. Don't overcomplicate the problem by creating theoretical relationships or explanations that will warp time or space. These are normal problems rooted in reality. It's just that the applicable relationship or explanation may not be readily apparent and you have to figure things out. Use your common sense to interpret anything that isn't clear.

Prefixes

If you're having trouble with a word in the question or answer choices, try dissecting it. Take advantage of every clue that the word might include. Prefixes and suffixes can be a huge help. Usually they allow you to determine a basic meaning. Pre- means before, post- means after, pro - is positive, de- is negative. From these prefixes and suffixes, you can get an idea of the general meaning of the word and try to put it into context. Beware though of any traps. Just because con- is the opposite of pro-, doesn't necessarily mean congress is the opposite of progress!

Hedge Phrases

Watch out for critical hedge phrases, led off with words such as "likely," "may," "can," "sometimes," "often," "almost," "mostly," "usually," "generally," "rarely," and "sometimes." Question writers insert these hedge phrases to cover every possibility. Often an answer choice will be wrong simply because it leaves no room for exception. Unless the situation calls for them, avoid answer choices that have definitive words like "exactly," and "always."

Switchback Words

Stay alert for "switchbacks." These are the words and phrases frequently used to alert you to shifts in thought. The most common switchback word is "but." Others include "although," "however," "nevertheless," "on the other hand," "even though," "while," "in spite of," "despite," and "regardless of."

New Information

Correct answer choices will rarely have completely new information included. Answer choices typically are straightforward reflections of the material asked about and will directly relate to the question. If a new piece of information is included in an answer choice that doesn't even seem to relate to the topic being asked about, then that answer choice is likely incorrect. All of the information needed to answer the question is usually provided for you in the question. You should not have to make guesses that are unsupported or choose answer choices that require unknown information that cannot be reasoned from what is given.

Time Management

On technical questions, don't get lost on the technical terms. Don't spend too much time on any one question. If you don't know what a term means, then odds are you aren't going to get much further since you don't have a dictionary. You should be able to immediately recognize whether or not you know a term. If you don't, work with the other clues that you have—the other answer choices and terms provided—but don't waste too much time trying to figure out a difficult term that you don't know.

Contextual Clues

Look for contextual clues. An answer can be right but not the correct answer. The contextual clues will help you find the answer that is most right and is correct. Understand the context in which a phrase or statement is made. This will help you make important distinctions.

Don't Panic

Panicking will not answer any questions for you; therefore, it isn't helpful. When you first see the question, if your mind goes blank, take a deep breath. Force yourself to mechanically go through the steps of solving the problem using the strategies you've learned.

Pace Yourself

Don't get clock fever. It's easy to be overwhelmed when you're looking at a page full of questions, your mind is full of random thoughts and feeling confused, and the clock is ticking down faster than you would like. Calm down and maintain the pace that you have set for yourself. As long as you are on track by monitoring your pace, you are guaranteed to have enough time for yourself. When you get to the last few minutes of the test, it may seem like you won't have enough time left, but if you only have as many questions as you should have left at that point, then you're right on track!

Answer Selection

The best way to pick an answer choice is to eliminate all of those that are wrong, until only one is left and confirm that is the correct answer. Sometimes though, an answer choice may immediately look right. Be careful! Take a second to make sure that the other choices are not equally obvious. Don't make a hasty mistake. There are only two times that you should stop before checking other answers. First is when you are positive that the answer choice you have selected is correct. Second is when time is almost out and you have to make a quick guess!

Check Your Work

Since you will probably not know every term listed and the answer to every question, it is important that you get credit for the ones that you do know. Don't miss any questions through careless mistakes. If at all possible, try to take a second to look back over your answer selection and make sure you've selected the correct answer choice and haven't made a costly careless mistake (such as marking an answer choice that you didn't mean to mark). The time it takes for this quick double check should more than pay for itself in caught mistakes.

Beware of Directly Quoted Answers

Sometimes an answer choice will repeat word for word a portion of the question or reference section. However, beware of such exact duplication. It may be a trap! More than likely, the correct choice will paraphrase or summarize a point, rather than being exactly the same wording.

Slang

Scientific sounding answers are better than slang ones. An answer choice that begins "To compare the outcomes..." is much more likely to be correct than one that begins "Because some people insisted..."

Extreme Statements

Avoid wild answers that throw out highly controversial ideas that are proclaimed as established fact. An answer choice that states the "process should used in certain situations, if..." is much more likely to be correct than one that states the "process should be discontinued completely." The first is a calm rational statement and doesn't even make a definitive, uncompromising stance, using a hedge word "if" to provide wiggle room, whereas the second choice is a radical idea and far more extreme.

Answer Choice Families

When you have two or more answer choices that are direct opposites or parallels, one of them is usually the correct answer. For instance, if one answer choice states "x increases" and another answer choice states "x decreases" or "y increases," then those two or three answer choices are very similar in construction and fall into the same family of answer choices. A family of answer choices consists of two or three answer choices, very similar in construction, but often with directly opposite meanings. Usually the correct answer choice will be in that family of answer choices. The "odd man out" or answer choice that doesn't seem to fit the parallel construction of the other answer choices is more likely to be incorrect.

How to Overcome Test Anxiety

The very nature of tests caters to some level of anxiety, nervousness, or tension, just as we feel for any important event that occurs in our lives. A little bit of anxiety or nervousness can be a good thing. It helps us with motivation, and makes achievement just that much sweeter. However, too much anxiety can be a problem, especially if it hinders our ability to function and perform.

"Test anxiety," is the term that refers to the emotional reactions that some test-takers experience when faced with a test or exam. Having a fear of testing and exams is based upon a rational fear, since the test-taker's performance can shape the course of an academic career. Nevertheless, experiencing excessive fear of examinations will only interfere with the test-taker's ability to perform and chance to be successful.

There are a large variety of causes that can contribute to the development and sensation of test anxiety. These include, but are not limited to, lack of preparation and worrying about issues surrounding the test.

Lack of Preparation

Lack of preparation can be identified by the following behaviors or situations:

Not scheduling enough time to study, and therefore cramming the night before the test or exam
Managing time poorly, to create the sensation that there is not enough time to do everything
Failing to organize the text information in advance, so that the study material consists of the entire text and not simply the pertinent information